THE BOOK O

Brittany Nightshade

Copyright © 2020 Brittany Nightshade

All rights reserved. This book or any portion thereof may not be reproduced or used in any manner whatsoever without the express written permission of the publisher except for the use of brief quotations in a book review.

Table of Contents

Preface: 7
Spell Craft, Ritual Work, and Intention..........................9
Calling Quarters and Elements 13
Casting a Circle 15
Elemental Circle Casting Ritual....................................16
White Magic..18
    Moon Water 18
    Moon Phases...20
    Sea Water..22
    Sage Cleansing (Smudging)..23
    Invocation of Hecate 24
    Invocation of Nyx, Goddess of Night 27
    Bonding with a Familiar..30
    Black Salt 31
    Jar Spells 32
    Protection Jar 34
    Home Protection Crystal Enchantment.......................35
    Confidence Tea Ritual...36
    Ancestral Communion..37
    To Find Closure..39
    Clairvoyance Spell 40
    To Bless a Relationship 41
    Rune of Protection 42

Protection Potion 43

Protection from Storms 44

Calming Spell 45

Spell of Protection 46

Old and Grey 47

Financial Prosperity 48

Remove Evil from an Object 49

Healing a Broken Heart 51

Witch Bottle (Curse Removal/Protection) 52

Chant to Bring Rain 53

Banishing Spell 54

Banishment Sigil 56

Protection Stone 57

Goal Accomplishment Jar Spell 58

Aphrodite Beauty Oil 60

To Prevent Nightmares 61

Basic Healing Spell 62

Pentacle Ward Spell 62

Cleansing/Charging a New Wand 63

Garden Growth Spell 64

Second Sight, Third Eye Ritual 65

Ritual of Undoing 67

Red Magic 69

Honey Jar 70

- Love Bell 71
- Candle Carving Ritual 72
- Aphrodite Sea Charm 73
- Adoration Candle Spell 74
- Hathor's Bath Ritual 76
- Attraction Poppet 77
- Love Knot 79
- Birch Bark Love Spell 79
- Reverse Love Spell (Undoing) 81
- A Seduction Spell 82
- Aphrodisiac Potion 83
- Aphrodisiac Bath 84
- Passion Tea 85

Black Magic 86
- Shadow Circle 87
- Invocation of Lyssa, Goddess of Rage 89
- Sour Jar 90
- Effigy Poppet Curse 92
- Ring of Power Enchantment 94
- Nightmare Jar 96
- Stone of Sorrow 97
- Stone of Jinxing 98
- Poppet Curse of Slight Pain 98
- Binding by Fear 99

Evil Eye Enchantment 101
Bones of Anger 102
Succubae's Lament (Dream Invasion) 103
Summon a Storm 104
Three Nights of Hell 106
A Seduction Spell 107
Severed Love 108
Discord and Darkness 110
Tattered Hearts Part 1 112
Tattered Hearts Part 2 113
Doll of Pain 113
Carman's Hex 115
Vanity and Insanity 115
Pepper Pentacle 117
Bad Luck Potion 118
Forbidden Death Curse 119

Sigil Magic 121
Divination 126
Rune Casting 127
Three Norns Method 128
Scrying 130
Pendulum Dowsing 131

The Futhark Runes 133
Notes **180**

In Closing 186

Preface:

Hello and merry meet! My name is Brittany Nightshade and I've spent many years studying witchcraft and pagan traditions. While on my journey, I've kept a record of the rituals and anything magical I've learned along the way in my personal book of shadows. I've taken parts from that book to create a public book of shadows for anyone interested in what I've learned and dispel common myths about witchcraft which are sometimes used to gatekeep and exclude people from the practice.

This book contains a wide assortment of magic spells, rituals, and information for practitioners of any level. There is also a section on divination with a guide to the Futhark Runes. These runes have been used for over a thousand years to prophesize and better understand our world and our place within it.

Whether you use these spells to craft your own rituals or use them as they are, remember the power is inside of you. There is no requirement to use exact recipes and from my experience personalizing a spell only makes it stronger because it's all about being able to focus and set your intentions. If a ritual in this book calls for a certain god or goddess and you don't feel a connection with that deity, you are free to change it to anything that helps you conduct your ritual more effectively. Only through meditation and practice will your powers grow so learn as much as you can and don't be afraid of making mistakes or not having the perfect ritual. It's all about you and your energies!

I wish you the best of luck in all your magical endeavors!
–Brittany Nightshade

Spell Craft, Ritual Work, and Intention

The first thing that comes to many people's minds when they hear the word 'witch' is magic. Unfortunately, most people have been misinformed of what magic is as it pertains to witchcraft.

The common misconceptions that have plagued history insinuate that witches have the ability to transmute humans into animals, shapeshift, control fire and lightning with their minds, disappear and reappear at will, levitate, and every other Hollywood trope you can imagine. While this might have been entertaining and at times stoked fears that go back thousands of years, the reality is much more down to earth and pragmatic in nature.

A witch's magic is more akin to what most would call 'prayer.' It might come as a shock that many witches also refer to their ritual work as prayer. After all, what is a prayer, but a ritual done with the aim of working with a deity or the cosmos to achieve a desired outcome?

Witches use magic to accomplish a number of things. Magic can protect, bewitch, influence, boost confidence, and imbue energies into charms, talismans and other mundane objects. It can alter the threads of fate and be used to honor and revere our gods, goddesses, ancestors, and the many other facets of nature.

It should be said that rituals and spells aren't necessarily the same thing. Spells usually involve some sort of ritual, but rituals don't always involve spell work/magic. Magic spells are done to achieve an outcome, such as healing from heartbreak or binding an abusive person. We achieve these outcomes through meditation and the direction of our intentions to affect the world around us. To aid in the proper direction and channeling of our intention and energies we generally employ ritual work.

However, ritual work doesn't always have to involve trying to receive or affect something. We also use rituals to honor and commune with our deities or with nature itself, depending on your chosen path. This is integral to most witches as they bond with their gods and goddesses and grow in power through their faith and dedication.

A witch's spell might be said over a boiling cauldron like you see in the movies, but it is more likely that witchcraft involves a ceremony that can be performed in nature, on the witch's home altar, in their kitchen, or in a coven setting. The place that works best for you is the one that allows you to achieve maximum concentration and connection with the spirit world.

Spells might be cast to affect the castor, other people, or to influence energies to cause some sort of change and can be beneficial or harmful. Spells that are positive in nature are often called blessings, while negative spells are generally called hexes or curses. Spells can also be used to prevent something from happening. These are called binding spells and can be positive or negative in nature depending on the intent.

The classification of certain magics as white, black, positive, negative, grey, etc., is hotly debated in the wider Wiccan community. Many argue that the intent of the practitioner is what gives a spell or ritual its designation, while many others argue that magic is magic, and we're not meant to try to put ritual work into boxes. Most traditional Wiccans take a no-nuance approach to any magic that affects or influences the will of another and considers them a violation of the Wiccan rede. On the other hand, many Eclectic Witches believe you must look at each situation on a case-by-case basis to determine whether the spell is justified. You may have your own way of determining this and morality is subjective. I choose to consult with The Norns, the Norse Goddesses of Fate, before I set out to make any changes in the world with my ritual work and I regularly consult with Hecate on day to day matters and self-development, I do this through meditative prayer and divination.

A ritual typically has a formula that the practitioner has crafted or received from another witch or their coven. It's quite common, and many have argued beneficial, to adapt a ritual to fit your needs. Spells can involve incantations, imagery, runes, candles, and other magical tools. Offerings are commonly made to the practitioner's god or goddess as part of a ritual ceremony of reverence.

There are many methods to cast spells. You might inscribe runes or sigils onto an object, like a ring or a necklace, to imbue it with certain properties. You could burn the picture of a romantic interest as part of the ritual for a love spell. You can even brew up a potion to use in your bath to make yourself more charismatic. There are virtually countless ways to go about crafting a spell. The most important part is that you feel a connection with what you're doing because that's the secret to successful spell crafting. Uncertainty and doubt are usually the reason for a spells failure, confidence is key, know that the details aren't as important as you directing your energies where they need to go through visualization and manifestation.

Ritual work and spell casting doesn't have to be complicated. A ritual can be as simple as lighting a candle or incense while thinking about the safety and protection of your family. For day-to-day spells, such as blessings, self-help, positive thoughts and the sending of helpful healing energies to others, it is not necessary to undertake the cumbersome task of a full circle-casting ritual. Although these intricacies can be useful for beginners in helping with concentration and immersion. To honor your ancestors, you could simply set them a place at the table with offerings of food and wine. Before bed, you can speak to your goddess and give her thanks for all the blessings she bestows upon your life. Just do what makes you feel good and what you think is the best way to worship and establish a connection to the magical world.

Calling Quarters and Elements

In witchcraft the Quarters refer to the elements of nature. These elements are forces that are revered by many pagans. They might be called by another name, but you will commonly hear them referred to as elements, elementals, watchtowers, corners, or quarters. These different terms might have slightly different meanings depending on the practitioner, but they all have a similar role in witchcraft.

The pentacle represents the four elements. The divine, or the practitioner, is the top point of the pentacle with the four elements making up the side points. This represents how the practitioner, or the divine within the practitioner, guides and acts as a conduit for the elemental forces. This is the most common interpretation, although views might differ from witch to witch, but as a general rule most witches incorporate the elements into their rituals in one way or another.

The four corners refer to the cardinal points of the compass: north, south, east and west. They might also refer to the four classical elements: water, earth, fire, and air. A fifth element that is often included in some Eastern traditions is 'The Void', or that which we can't see. Most western traditions consider the self, or the spirit, to be the fifth.

Many techniques are derived from different traditions and a witch may try different things or adapt and create their own rituals until they find something that works for them. The tradition of witchcraft spans across many different cultures and is a constantly evolving, living belief which is why you will find such variation in practice.

Many witches make use of the elements, seeing them as inter-connected energies that make up everything we see and experience. Practitioners will often call the Guardians of the Watchtowers to keep the energies stable and unaffected while channeling. As you develop your powers you'll likely have your own unique way of channeling the elements. In the next section I'll go over different methods that you could use and adapt to cast your own circle.

Casting a Circle

Witches may cast a circle to prepare a magical, sacred space to meditate, cast a spell or perform a ritual. The circles are actually spheres that are used as a type of insulation from unwanted energies which might affect the spell, ritual, or meditation. This helps prevent the misdirection of intention during spell work or the interruption of energy transference. Circles aren't necessary, but in my opinion, can greatly aid in concentration.

A circle can be cast by simply holding out your finger, wand, athame or staff and turning 360 degrees in a clockwise motion. The circle can be closed after you are done by doing the same but in reverse (counterclockwise) or by cutting the boundary of the circle with your athame, wand, or hand. This is an easy and effective way to cast a circle, but you might also wish to incorporate an invocation or ritual of your own design. It doesn't matter how you cast your circle; the key is having faith in what you are doing so you can effectively use your energy to create the barrier.

A popular method of casting a circle involves incorporating the elements and cardinal directions into the casting. For example, you might want to place an object representing each element in each direction you will be pointing to while casting the circle or call upon the guardians and elements themselves. The following are examples of what might be used to represent each element, but you may use anything that you personally associate with the element.

Air/East: sword, athame, wand, feathers, bells, ribbons, Ace of Swords Tarot.

Fire/South: candles, thorns, wands and other phallic objects, dragons, matches, masculine aspect, Ace of Wands Tarot.

Water/West: chalice, cup, seashells, crystal ball, ankh, mirror, water/wine, feminine aspect, Ace of Cups Tarot.

Earth/North: pentacle, altar, metals, coins, flowers/herbs, soil, sand, salt, nuts and seeds, Ace of Pentacles Tarot.

Elemental Circle Casting Ritual

Prepare the area in which you wish to cast your circle, you can place objects representing the elements at their corresponding cardinal direction. With your wand or other tool in your dominant hand point towards the east side of the circle and say the following:

"I call upon the Guardian of the East, Element of Air, to watch over this sacred space."

Envision the Guardian appearing in the east, bow to acknowledge the Guardian, and turn to the south. With your hand extended say the following:

"I call upon the Guardian of the South, Element of Fire, to watch over this sacred space."

Envision the Guardian, bow to acknowledge him, and turn to the west. With your hand extended say the following:

"I call upon the Guardian of the West, Element of Water, to watch over this sacred space."

As you envision the arrival of the Guardian, bow in respect, and turn to the north. With your arm still extended, say the following:

"I call upon the Guardian of the North, Element of Earth, to watch over this sacred space."

Raise your hand up into the air and say the following:

"I call upon the spirit to protect this space, as I will, the circle is cast."

White Magic

Magic doesn't necessarily have an official color system, but people usually will describe it as white or light if the spell doesn't harm or influence the will of another. White Magic is the safest of all spell types and is a good place to start if you're a beginner because there's no potentially negative consequences to misdirecting your intention.

Healing and protection rituals are some of the oldest spells known. Healers were integral parts of pagan villages and their studies in herbalism and health are what went on to become modern medicine. These spells are an important part of any witch's arsenal and will prepare you for anything you encounter on your path.

Moon Water

Moon water is used in spells, potions, cleansing and charging sigils: pretty much any witchcraft practice where you use water and need the power and protection of the moon. This water can also be placed on your altar and used as a representation of the Element of Water and the moon. The only essential part of a ritual to make moon water is the presence of the moon in the night sky. You can simply place your jar in a windowsill or do a complex ritual invoking a deity.

You will need:

One clear glass jar or bottle with lid

Water

A place to safely place your jar outside at night

Fill your container with water and place it outside or in a window once the moon has risen in the sky. You may say a prayer to any gods or goddesses of your choosing if you so wish - this is especially helpful if you plan on using your water in a ritual involving said deities. Common Lunar Goddesses you might want to call to are Selene, Artemis, Hecate, Diana, Bastet, Luna, Astarte, or Phoebe.

Example Moon Water Blessing Ritual calling upon Hecate:

Say the following in the presence of the moon once the sun is completely out of sight.

"I call upon the Grace of Hecate,

I ask of you to grant your blessings and power to me on this night of most importance.

Fill me and my Lunar Water with your divine grace so that I may fulfill my purposes and bring blinding clarity into the darkness as you have always done."

Place your jar out for an hour or so or retrieve it in the morning, don't worry about the jar coming into contact with sunlight as your intention was to charge the jar with moonlight and the suns light can't simply undo that.

Moon Phases

Moon water can be charged under any phase of the moon and different phases can be used for different types of moon water, although it's not necessary. These phases and their strengths can be applied to your other spell work as well.

Full moon: healing, charging, banishing, love magic, cleansing, protection

Waning gibbous: cleansing, relinquishing, undoing curses and bindings

Last quarter: breaking curses and bad habits, banishing, relinquishing

Waning crescent: success, curing illness, attaining wisdom, balance, atonement

Dark moon: soul searching, banishing, divination, deconstruction, binding

Waxing crescent: wealth, luck, constructive magic, friendship, attraction, success

First quarter: motivation, divination, calming, strength, growth

Waxing gibbous: success, good health, attraction, motivation

New moon: new relationships, love, new beginnings, change, liminal spaces

Sea Water

Sea/ocean water can be used by a witch for a myriad of things. It's great for cleansing and can be used in a spray bottle or as a bath for any magic or mundane objects. You can also set a jar or bottle of it on your altar to represent both Water and Earth elements.

It's not always easy to collect your own sea water, but fortunately you can make some yourself that's just as effective. You can work with any god/goddess with dominion over the sea. In this ritual, I'll be working with Amphitrite, the wife of Poseidon, but you can also work with Hecate who is also honored and worshiped as a sea goddess.

What you will need:
Hot water (2 cups)
Seashell
Sea salt (4 pinches)
Container for mixing

Mix your sea salt and water until all the salt is dissolved. Hold your seashell in your hand and loudly say the following:

"Amphitrite! Queen of the Sea!
I ask that you lend your power to this vessel!
Mighty goddess of the deep!
I welcome you and give you thanks!"

Drop your shell into the water and the ritual is complete.

Remember to give thanks to your god or goddess when using your sea water.

Sage Cleansing (Smudging)

You can cleanse anything with the smoke from sage. This is either done with a sage stick (smudge stick) or by burning sage in an incense burner. Sage has powerful cleansing properties and can be used to cleanse your home, altar space, jewelry, crystals, candles or any other ritual tool or object. Sage can also be used to cleanse yourself. Other common incense used for cleansing are myrrh and dragons blood, but I typically use sage. (Make sure that your sage is ethically sourced, many big box chain stores get their sage for unsustainable sources that harm the areas in which they're harvested. This is especially important if you're using white sage. I highly suggest growing your own, it's easy and will strengthen your connection nature.

To cleanse your home set your intention to cleanse, light your sage and allow it to burn out and smolder. Carry the sage throughout the house and allow the smoke to flow into the rooms. Pay special attention to mirrors, hallways, and other high traffic areas. As you do this you can say a prayer to a goddess or an incantation to better focus your intention.

To cleanse an object, do the same thing: set your intention, light your sage and run the object through the smoke. If the object is large, take the sage and move it around the object, letting the smoke envelope it.

To cleanse yourself, light your sage and allow it to burn out, take the smoke with your hands and direct it around your body. "Wash" your hands, face, body, legs, etc. with the smoke. Do this with the intent of cleansing and purification.

Invocation of Hecate

Devotion and Dedication Ritual

Hecate is the mother of all witches and the Greek goddess of witchcraft, magic, and the sea. She holds the keys to the underworld and can equally protect from the spirits of the underworld or send them to attack. She's known as a liminal goddess, meaning she freely crosses between realms of Earth, Heaven and Hades, and can walk through the veil that separates the three. Hecate is known as the Triple Moon Goddess and holds dominion over the Earth, Heavens and Sea, and wields immeasurable power as a daughter of Titans and the matron goddess of witches.

If you acquire her favor, she will shield you from the unjust and bring you creativity, wisdom, and guidance. She is darkness. She is everything. As you develop a relationship with her you will find that the knowledge and wisdom needed to bring forth light resides in the mysteries and blessings of the dark.

It helps if you are in a meditative state when calling out to her, but you do not have to be. I find my connection to her to be strongest at night. Since she represents all phases of the moon it doesn't have to be at a certain time of month, but the new moon is ideal. It would help if you incorporate one or more of her symbols. For instance, some of Hecate's symbols are the moon, keys, black, silver, darkness, crossroads, the number three, and dogs. There are many more and you should learn about each individually and why they represent her as that will strengthen your connection and understanding of her. Place these items on your altar or hold them during the invocation.

Focus on the symbol and what it represents, open up your mind and be willing to accept her energies. If possible, light a black candle. Place offerings such as wine, food or incense on your altar or ritual space. Common offerings to Hecate are honey, fish, garlic, eggs, and wine. You should always make offerings to show your thanks and dedication when you work with Hecate. Offerings can simply be placed upon your altar or workspace and you can do with them what you wish after the ritual is concluded although some people like to leave wine on their altars until some of the liquid has evaporated.

The following prayer is an invocation I've created to call upon Hecate and devote oneself to her path. You can use my ritual or develop your own devotional ritual just as you can for any of the invocations in this book.

Clear your thoughts and let the image fill your mind, then begin to relax. Concentrate on your energy connecting with the darkness, feel your energies being aligned with hers and say the following:

"Hecate, Mother of Darkness, I call upon you!
I am answering your call and am ready to dedicate myself to your path!
Goddess of Night, protect me with your arcane power!
Grant me the sight to see through the veil and attain the wisdom you grant!
Maiden of thresholds and crossroads surround me in your darkness so that I can bring forth my light!
Dark Mother! I pledge my loyalty!
I honor you now and forever! By the power of the Triple Moon!

Hail Hecate! Hail Hecate! Hail Hecate! "

As your relationship with Hecate develops, you'll find your own way of worshiping and communicating with her. Each relationship is different and deeply personal. She can be demanding but will never fault or punish you for your shortcomings so never hesitate to seek her out and let her torch guide you through any turmoil you may face.

Pray/commune with Hecate regularly. I normally hold a ritual on the new moon and give thanks and offerings daily. Cherish the bond you have with her as her grace will be a blessing that will protect and lead you through the void.

Invocation of Nyx, Goddess of Night

Nyx is the primordial Goddess of Night. She is a daughter of Chaos and has been here since the beginning of time itself. It is said that even the mighty Zeus feared her. This ritual is meant to create a bond with this ancient goddess of unfathomable power.

You will need:
Blessing oil

Altar
Full moon drawn on an altar cover
Sage
Sweet grass
Red rose petals
1 red candle
1 blue candle
1 purple candle
1 black candle
1 white candle

Smudge the altar, the candles, and yourself with the sage. Anoint your candles with the oil and place the sage on the altar (use a fireproof vessel or plate for the sage). Place the five candles on the altar with black in the north, white in the east, red in the south, and blue in the west with purple in the middle. Light them in this order: black, white, red, blue, purple.

Say the following:

"Nyx, great Goddess of the Night!
Lover of Erebus, mother of Moros, Thanatos, Hypnos, Charon, Nemesis, and the Fates, I ask you to accept my loyalty and my love as your follower and servant. I ask for your protection and guidance, bringer of the night, I ask for your wisdom and blessings."

Re-light the sage if it burnt out and light up the sweet grass (if you don't have sweet grass you can use any other type of incense). Use the sweet grass to smudge the altar, the candles, the rose petals, and yourself. Place the sweet grass next to the sage and let it burn out as you visualize Nyx sending you her protection, wisdom, guidance, and blessing. Once the sweet grass and the sage burn out sprinkle the petals into the gaps between the candles and the herbs from your hands as you chant:

"I am [your name]. I am a Priest/Priestess for my Goddess, you, Nyx, if you will have me.

This is my request, and these are my words.

May this oath stay strong, my faith never wavers, my love never weakens.

Blessings of Nyx, wash over me!"

Honor Nyx with offerings and prayer and she will always answer your call. There are many gods and goddesses, I suggest learning about as many as you can and find the ones that resonate with your personal energies. Spend time learning about them and make your own rituals using inspiration from the invocations in this book or craft your own from scratch! I would imagine any god or goddess would be impressed with someone who took the time to craft their own ritual for them, don't worry about the details, it's literally the thought that counts.

Bonding with a Familiar

A familiar is an animal or nature spirit that you can bond with that can assist you in your practice. Familiars can lend you their energies and protect against malevolent forces. Some bonds happen naturally but you can also perform a ritual to attempt to create a familiar bond.

Embrace the animal or envision the spirit you wish to bond with and say the following:

"A bond to be made in (god, goddess, or entities) name,
I ask for your assistance,
Keep me safe from all that'd harm,
And counter all resistance.
Together we can do great things,
No matter what the 'morrow brings."

Meditate on the connection between your spirit and theirs: you will feel the connection when it's made. If the spell didn't work keep in mind that not every spirit wants to or is ready to be your familiar and you stand a much greater chance if you have already built a connection with spirit you are trying to enlist. As you grow in experience you might find that familiars will call to you and your ability to bond with them will grow.

Black Salt

Black salt is an ingredient that is commonly used in witchcraft and can be made from simple household items. Black salt is a powerful protective ingredient and tool that can be used as part of any greater ritual that calls for any kind of salt or simply spread around the home or kept in a sachet for protection.

You will need:
Sea salt
Ashes

The simplest way to make black salt is to take some ashes from your incense burner or fireplace and grind 2 parts salt with 1 parts ash. As you mix the ingredients, be sure to charge the salt with protective intent.

You may also add other protective ingredients such as eggshells, cinnamon, or a pinch of ethically acquired graveyard dirt. When acquiring graveyard dirt be sure to leave an offering such as tobacco, salt or sugar.

Jar Spells

Jar spells are an old form of folk magic that can be done in a variety of ways for a near limitless number of purposes. The maker sets/defines their intent and places charged objects into a jar. The jar is then sealed and ceremoniously discarded. Protection jars are typically buried or hidden away although some spells call for the destruction of the jar. The specifics of the jars aren't important: the intent and your focus are what makes everything work.

The first step is to define and set your intentions, know exactly what you want and keep focused. You can also write your intention on a piece of paper to be placed in the jar during the ritual. You then fill your jar with objects related to your intent, such as crystals, spices, herbs, liquids and anything else you wish to use.

Place the items in one by one, charge each item by focusing your intent into them as you place them into the jar. After everything is in the jar, you must seal it so the energies within the bottle are contained. You can do this by dripping candle wax on the seal or letting the candle burn down onto the jar. If your lid is plastic, you'll need to place fireproof paper between the candle and lid. You can also use string, glue, honey, or anything else that would work to keep the jar energetically sealed.

The jar can now be buried, destroyed or hidden away so they may work their magic. You can also make small jars and carry them with you. I keep a small protection jar with me whenever I leave the house.

Protection Jar

This jar will work to protect the maker or anyone they focus their intentions on while crafting it. Change up the ingredients to fit your own style if you'd like. I use ingredients that are generally known for their protective qualities.

You will need:
Jar
White candle
Dirt or sand
Crystal (quartz or black tourmaline)
White pepper
Basil leaf
Cinnamon (powder or stick)
Shell

Cleanse your ingredients and place them on your altar or ritual space with your jar.

Meditate on your intent for a moment, for example, the need to be safe and protected from harm. If you're seeking protection from a specific thing, concentrate on that thing and its inability to hurt you.

Maintain your focus as you pour the dirt or sand into your jar. This is your base. Continue to place each item in one at a time all while directing your energies and intent into the items.

Light the white candle and allow the wax to drip on the seal of the jar. You may also place the candle on top of the jar and let it completely burn down, coating the jar in wax.

The jar can now be hidden away or buried. The jar could be placed behind a wall, in the back of a closet, under your bed or even built into the walls of your house. If your jar is small enough you can even carry it with you.

Home Protection Crystal Enchantment

You will need:
Large crystal
Large bowl or cauldron
Water
Sea salt
Basil
Something from your home/yard
Wand or something to stir the water

Place your crystal in the cauldron and fill it with enough water to cover the crystal. Throw a pinch of salt into the cauldron and say the following:

> *"Bless this family and bless this home,*
> *While we're here and while we roam,*
> *When darkness beckons our light will shine,*
> *And protect the ones that I call mine."*

Throw in a pinch of basil and something from your yard or home. It can be a rock, a leaf, a blade a grass or even a fiber from your carpet. Stir with wand something that has a connection to the property you are blessing.

Use your wand to stir the water in a clockwise motion. Do 7 complete circles around the crystal while stirring.

Display the crystal in a common area of the home.

Confidence Tea Ritual

This is a simple morning tea ritual to get your positive energy flowing and to set our intentions for the day.

You will need:

Your favorite type of tea
Your favorite teacup

Brew the tea and pour into your favorite cup while saying the following:

"Confident, beautiful, secure and grand,
I hold the future in the palm of my hand,
I'll conquer the day and reap the rewards,
While always moving forever forwards."

Relax and drink your tea while thinking of all the things you're going to accomplish today.

Ancestral Communion

The reverence of our ancestors is a common part of many pagan practices, we honor our ancestors and reach out to them for guidance. Use this ritual to open up a spiritual link between you and your ancestors.

You will need:
Athame (ritual dagger)
White candle
Ansuz rune

Offerings

Inscribe the rune onto the candle with your athame. Light the candle and sit in a comfortable position. Place your offerings in front of you or on your altar. Meditate on the Futhark rune, Ansuz, which is used in Ancestral Magic. Allow the rune to open up a connection to the person you are trying to connect with.

For as long as you see fit, meditate on the person you are trying to contact. Pay homage to this person's life and reminisce on any memories you have of them.

Say the following incantation:

"I feel the warmth of your body and soul.
I welcome you here, my heart is whole.
Please come to me, (optional: insert name)."

If the person has answered your call, you will feel their presence. You may get a chill or even feel warmth depending on the circumstances.

You will likely just feel their energy, but if you are experienced enough, it's possible to hear or even see them. It's also quite common after an invitation is made for them to visit you in your dreams where communication is much easier. If the spell isn't successful, try it once again before going to sleep.

Use this ritual to honor your ancestors. Consider setting a place at your dining table with the offerings as part of the ritual. Enjoy their presence and give thanks for their protections and blessings. Speak with them and listen to what they have to say. After you've made contact and accomplished what you set out to do make sure to thank them for coming and tell them that you both must be on your way.

To Find Closure

This ritual is meant to help you find closure after a relationship has come to an end. This can be a romantic relationship or a friendship that has gone sour. Sometimes our past weighs heavy on our minds and this ritual can be a great way to put your first foot forward down a new path with new opportunities.

You will need:
Red candle
Blue candle
Black candle
Incense

Light the candles and the incense and say the following:

"As you leave my life, I leave behind my pain.
As you scatter like dust, So does all my hurt.

As I leave you in my past, I leave with you my sorrow."

Take a moment to reflect on how much you've learned and grown since before the relationship. Imagine how you'll use this knowledge going forward and starting a new chapter in your life, better prepared and wiser than you ever were before.

Clairvoyance Spell

This spell will allow you to see people's true intentions and will give you the power to see through any illusion or manipulation.

You will need:
Amber incense
Blue candle

Light the candle and the incense and say the following:

"Veritas, Goddess of Truth!
Grant me the power to see through the lies,
To see the intention in everyone's eyes,
Deception be damned, illusions be gone
A sight that can be counted on"

Make sure to give thanks to Veritas for your new fledgling gift of clairvoyance, work on this skill through meditation, this ritual can be repeated whenever you want as a ritual to Veritas. As your connection with Veritas grows your powers of clairvoyance will as well.

To Bless a Relationship

A simple ritual to do with your significant other to ensure a long-lasting and happy relationship.

You will need:
Loaf of bread
Wine glass
Othala rune

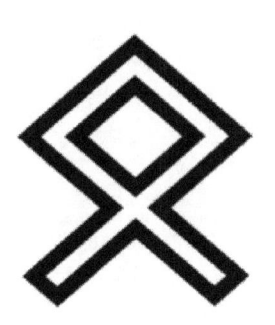

Bake a fresh loaf of bread. Hold it up to the moon and ask the gods and goddesses to bless the bread as well as the relationship. Break off a piece of the bread for your partner, as well as one for yourself, and fill the glass you'll be sharing with a beverage of your choice.

Incorporate the Othala rune in any way you'd like. You can etch or draw it onto the wine glass, bake it into the bread design or simply draw it on a piece of paper and use it as a coaster for the glass.

As you share time together, share the bread as well. Do not cut the bread with a knife or any other cutting tool. Just break off the pieces with your hands. The bread may be any type you like and you can add butter, jam, or anything else that you and your partner might like.

Rune of Protection

"Algiz, Rune of Life"

Algiz is a powerful rune of protection and can either be drawn on paper and placed or etched somewhere close, like on your altar, clothing, ritual tools, or your body. It can also be used in crafting your own protection spells. Algiz is one of the most common runes found amongst archeological finds in Scandinavia and was commonly placed on the shields of warriors before going into battle.

Protection Potion

This potion acts as a ward to any spirits with ill-intentions. Vervain has been used for centuries as a ward against vampires and works against any malicious spirit. Basil has also been used for protection against the evil eye, which is where someone is essentially casting negative energies at you with their gaze.

You will need:
1/2 cup of water
1 teaspoon vervain or 5 drops of vervain Oil
2 tablespoons sea salt
1 teaspoon of basil or 5 drops of basil oil
Glass jar

Lightly sprinkle the potion around your home in discreet places (i.e. in closets) and anoint the bottom of your shoes and those of your loved ones. This potion can also be used as a powerful ritual ingredient for any spells pertaining to protection.

Protection from Storms

This spell works to grant you and your loved ones safety from inclement weather. Thurisaz is a rune that represents loss, pain and hardship, we'll be reversing that rune to and using it in a ritual to ask that we be spared from those hardships.

"Thurisaz reversed"

With your dominant hand, write the reversed Thurisaz Rune in the air in the direction of the storm.

Say the following:

> *"Children of the winds, guardians of Air,*
> *Listen to my words, harken to my prayer.*
> *Breathe upon me gently, breathe upon me warm."*
> *Guard my home and family. Keep us safe from harm.*
> *In Thor's name,*
> *So Mote it Be!"*

Calming Spell

This is a simple spell to bring about calmness in oneself. Once this spell is mastered, it can even be used to calm those around you.

Look deeply at the palm of your hand and chant the following until you can feel the calm overtaking you, if you're in a public setting you can also chant the mantra in your mind:

*"As I look into my palm,
The goddess grants the gift of calm."*

As you repeat the mantra study the lines of your hands, see how the creases intersect, interconnected as all things are. Repeat until peace rushes over your body.

Spell of Protection

A basic protection spell that will help you focus and prevent the misdirection of your intentions. This spell is also useful for creating a barrier against the ill-will of others.

Draw a pentacle in front of you (pictured above).

Chant the following:

"By the power of the five-point star,
spirits be you near or far,
I call on thee, hear this cry,
spirits that protect come now and fly,
oh spirits now I ask of thee,
to protect me from dark energy,
so mote it be... so mote it be... so mote it be."

Old and Grey

This is a ritual to ensure that you and the one you love will outlast all the challenges life may throw at you. All obstacles can be overcome with a strong will and a bit of magic!

You will need:
Hair from you and your loved one
Small rose quartz
Small pouch

Place the hair and the rose quartz crystal into the pouch and say the following:

"Until the sun no longer shines,

Long life and health to me and mine,
The storms we'll weather,
the mountains we'll climb,
Our love will remain,
until the end of time."

Hold the pouch and meditate on the wonderful future you and your beloved will have. Keep the pouch in a safe place.

Financial Prosperity

This is a wealth spell that is designed to give you the strength and confidence you need to achieve success, while also asking the gods to send opportunities and show you the path to achieve your goals.

You will need:
Sage or jasmine incense
Yellow and green candle
Something representing your god/goddess

Light the candles on your altar on either side of your representation and say the following:

"Day by day, I waste away,

No time to wait, I can't delay,
Grant me the strength, to rise above,
Send opportunity and wealth my way."

Close your eyes, envision your future successes and meditate on how you'll go about achieving your goals. When you're ready to end the ritual, thank your god/goddess and blow out the candles.

Remove Evil from an Object

This ritual can be used to remove evil or cursed/negative energies or entities from any object.

You will need:
1 white candle
Salt
Cursed object
Pentacle
Black cloth
Tourmaline crystal

Set the object down on the black cloth and put the pentacle on top of it, if you can't put it on top of the object just make sure that it's touching it. Light the candle and put it in front of the object.

Take your salt and use it to draw a circle around your object, making sure the circle is as thick and perfect as you can make it, I like to make my salt circles about ½ an inch in thickness but as long as the circle is complete it will work.

Place the tourmaline so that's it bordering the circle of salt on the outside, during the ritual you'll be breaking the salt circle to open up a path to the crystal.

Say the following:

> *"Positive energy, stay with me,*
> *Negative energy leave me be.*
> *Leave, you don't belong here,*
> *Go far away, never near.*
> *I demand all evil to flee.*
> *I demand that you listen to me.*
> *Get out, get out, get out.*
> *Leave, leave. Hear my shout.*
> *This is my will so mote it be."*

Now clear out a path through the salt that leads to your tourmaline crystal, the cursed energies contained within the object will exit the circle and be neutralized by the tourmaline as it tries to escape.

Healing a Broken Heart

This is a ritual for healing a broken heart, ending a dying relationship, and starting anew. Do this spell under a full or new moon.

Call upon your goddess/god of choice and say the following chant until you feel the pain lift from your heart:

> *"Oh Goddess, take my pain,*
> *Steady as a falling rain.*
> *Give me courage to call an end,*
> *Give me a chance to start again.*
> *Help heal all the broken hearts,*
> *So that we may easily part.*
> *Oh, Goddess let my will be done,*
> *With no harm to anyone.*
> *Blessed Be! So mote it be!"*

Visualize yourself in your mind, happy, and ending with ease and starting new and fresh. See new beginnings and happy times with no more pain ahead for yourself.

Witch Bottle (Curse Removal/Protection)

Witch bottles have been used in folk magic for hundreds of years to break curses and protect the maker from another witches magical attack. They are a type of jar spell.

You will need:
Jar or bottle
Salt
Black candle
Something from the victim
Bent nails or pins
Urine or wine

Do this like any other jar spell. Focus your intention. In this instance, it's the removal of a curse or protection from magical attack. Place each object in one at a time. Start with the salt for your base followed by the item from you or the people you're trying to protect. This can be fingernails, hair, teeth, a picture or anything connected to them. Place your nails and/or pins in next, followed by the urine or wine.

Close the jar and seal it with the black candle wax. Bury the jar in your yard, concluding the ritual. This jar serves as a sort of decoy for any negative energies, trapping them beneath the earth and leaving you free from harm.

Chant to Bring Rain

This spell will utilize the Berkano rune to encourage growth in the surrounding flora. To be able to grow and flourish the surrounding plants will need water. Once you set these energies into motion it won't be long until rain finds its way to you to fulfill this need.

(Berkano, Rune of Growth)

Draw the Berkano rune in the ground outside and say the following:

> *"Goddess bring the rain down,*
> *Giving life unto the ground.*
> *Energy to feed the seed,*

Mother-natures gift to me.
Goddess bring the rain down,
Giving life unto the ground.
Energy to feed the seed,
And a healthy harvest bring.
As in my will, so mote it be!"

Banishing Spell (Spirit and Demon Banishment)

If you find you are being haunted by a spirit, demon, or other supernatural entity you will need to cast a banishing spell to rid yourself of their presence.

What you will need:
Enough salt to draw a pentacle.
Citrine crystal or selenite
A room with a window

Draw a pentacle on the ground or on your altar with the salt, place your crystal in the middle of the pentacle, open your window and chant the following three times:

> *"Ashes to ashes, dust to dust,*
> *Return from whence you came,*
> *You are no longer welcome, it's time to go,*
> *I do this in Hecate's name!"*

Close your window and remove the pentacle to complete the spell.

Banishment Sigil

If the previous spell didn't work and you can't seem to rid yourself of your unwanted spirits, you could try this sigil.

Dr. Johannes Faust wrote a book called *The Black Raven* on the summoning and binding of spirits in the early 1500s. In the pages of this manic document are many sigils that serve different purposes when summoning spirits. One of these sigils claims to have the power to banish evil spirits.

I've never personally had to resort to this method, but I found this sigil while researching and thought it was interesting and worth sharing.

It also goes without saying that you can create your own sigils for spirit banishment.

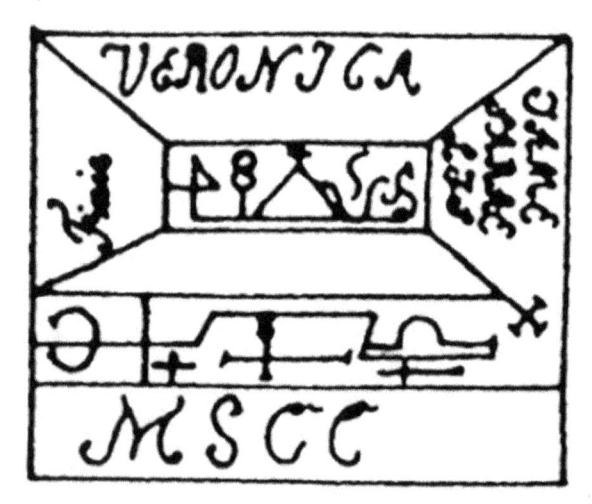

Faust's grimoire says to draw this sigil on a Monday during the hour of Jupiter, which for Mondays will be the 3rd hour of daylight, typically between 8 and 9 AM.

Protection Stone

Find a stone with a high vibration, to do this hold a stone in your hand and feel its energies. Take the stone outside and find a peaceful place to sit. Stare into the stone, ground yourself, and charge the rock with energy and intention. Say the following:

> *"Stone, evil shall you deny.*
> *Send it to the Earth and sky.*
> *Send it to the flame and sea,*
> *Stone of power, protect me."*

You can carry this stone with you, keep it in your home or give it to someone else to protect them.

Goal Accomplishment Jar Spell

This ritual is designed to keep one on a desired path, whether you're trying to quit a bad habit, studying for an exam, learning a new trade, dieting and exercise or any other number of goals you wish to accomplish.

You will need:

Dirt or sand

Pepper flakes (any kind will do)

Red candle

Bind rune of perseverance

Glass jar with lid

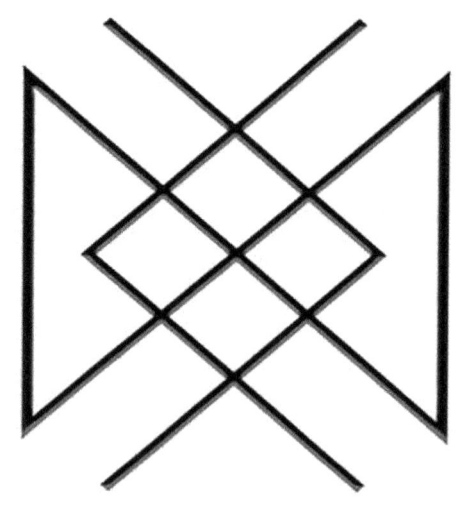

"bind rune of perseverance"

Focus on accomplishing your goal and carve the bind rune into the candle. This bind rune is a combination of the Dagaz and Othala Futhark runes. The Dagaz runes represents the daily cycles of life while Othala represents positive accumulated outcomes, generally wealth and status from the accomplishments of you and your ancestors.

Put your dirt into the jar as your base. Add a few dashes of pepper flakes into the jar. Light the red candle and meditate on your goals and how you will accomplish them. Drip some of the candle wax into the jar. You can speak your intentions to your god, goddess or spirit and ask them to aid you in achieving your goals. Give thanks to your deity and make an offering if you'd like.

Meditate on what your life will be like once you accomplish your task and see yourself transcended to this new position. Seal the jar with the wax and extinguish your candle to conclude the ritual.

Keep the jar in a safe place and don't open or dispose of it until you've achieved your goals or you no longer wish to pursue those goals.

Aphrodite Beauty Oil

Not only is this oil great for your hair and skin, but it will also gift you with the radiant blessings of Aphrodite! With this you'll want to follow the directions and not substitute any of the oils for others as some oils can damage your skin or hair if used in improper amounts. Jojoba and Almond are great bases for oil mixtures as they don't clog your pores and aren't harmful in any amounts, our additive will be lavender, which has been shown to promote hair growth and prevent thinning, it's also one of my favorite scents!

You will need:
2 Oz of jojoba or almond oil
5 drops of lavender oil
Glass bottle

Mix the oils together in the bottle and say the following:
"Aphrodite, bless this oil,
Elevate this mortal coil.
Radiant, shining, blissful beauty,
Proudly displayed for the world to see!"

Put a few drops into the palm of your hand and rub together. You can lightly apply this oil to your hair and skin to look, smell, and feel great!

To Prevent Nightmares

You will need:
3 white candles
teaspoon of spearmint leaves
Infuser (optional)
Hot water
Tea cup

Put the spearmint leaves into the glass and add the hot water.

Place the three candles in a triangle around the glass, with the glass in the center.

Say the following:
"I am safe while I sleep, there is nothing to fear.
For now I understand, nothing can hurt me in here."

Blow out the candles and drink the water, don't swallow any of the leaves, you can use a spearmint teabag or tea infuser to make things easier. Repeat this ritual every night for about a week, after that you can start spacing out your need to perform the ritual. Eventually you will be free of nightmares without the need of the ritual.

Basic Healing Spell

Place your hands near the site of the pain, palms facing the source of the pain. Close your eyes and envision the pain coming out as a small thread. Slightly and slowly pull your hand back as the thread follows. As you feel the energies in your palms building cast the energies up and away with a quick motion of your hand.

While this spell is basic and doesn't require much ritual, being able to perform it typically requires years of practice and meditation on the healing arts. Advanced practitioners can use this spell to heal others as well as themselves.

Pentacle Ward Spell

You will need:
Sage smudge stick
Sandalwood incense

Start by meditating until you reach the point of complete tranquility. You need to empty your mind of all negative thoughts and feelings. Place a stick of sandalwood incense in each room of your home. Pray to your deity for the protection of your home and family.

Light your smudge stick and start by tracing a pentacle in the air in the windows and doors of each room. Start at the lower left-hand part of the pentacle and imagine a dome forming over your home. This spell needs to be redone every month because the wards lose power over time. Finish by giving thanks to your favored god/goddesses.

Cleansing/Charging a New Wand

Wands allow us to better focus our intentions while spellcasting. Wands can carry residual energies from previous owners or the maker of the wand so it's always a good idea to do a cleansing ritual and charge it anew.

You will need:

Cauldron (or pot)

Sea saltwater

Incense

Quartz crystal

Wand to be cleansed

Flowers, gemstones and or rose quartz.

Boil water in the cauldron and mix in a dash of sea salt. Stir three times and say, "May the goddess enter the water, may the goddess make it pure." Leave the cauldron to cool in the garden (or a grassy area) in a sunny spot and say the following, "May Apollo's rays fill you with power".

Make a circle around your cauldron with the flowers and stones. Add a crystal to the cauldron or pot. It should take about an hour to cool. Light the incense and place the wand into the now cooled water. Say the following, "May Apollo's light be released!" Remove the wand from the water and stir the water three times clockwise.

Allow the wand to dry on your windowsill.

Garden Growth Spell

What you will need:
Amethyst or obsidian stone
Small bowl of water
Thorns (from a rose or other plant)
feather
Leaves or flower petals

Cast a circle around your garden by placing the stone on the north end of the garden to represent Earth, the feather to the East for Air, the thorns to the South for Fire, and the bowl of water to the West. After casting your circle spread the flowers/leaves within the circle.

Stand at the south end of your garden and face north, say the following:

"Earth, Air, Fire, Water, and spirit!
I call on thee to protect my garden and help it grow!
Spirit protect, Earth nourish, Water feed, Fire guard, and Air lift up!
Hear my call and come to me,
This is my will so mote it be."

Tend to your garden daily, give thanks to the elemental spirits that watch after your garden alongside you. Spend time in your garden and learn as much about it as you can, how it grows, breaths, and ebbs with cycles of the year. Respect your garden, treat it as an extension of your craft and it will reward you with a bountiful harvest.

Second Sight, Third Eye Ritual

Many ancient cultures and religions were aware of the third eye. They believed it to be related to a small eye-shaped endocrine gland in the brain called the pineal gland. The Eye of Horus is believed to be a representation of this gland, and it is also related to the root chakra in Hindu beliefs. This is a simple ritual to work on developing your third eye which will increase clairvoyance and overall magical abilities.

You will need:
Purple candle
Amethyst

I'll be using a purple candle as it represents the crown chakra and an amethyst as it is thought to stimulate the third eye.

Light your candle and/or incense and sit in a comfortable position. Hold the amethyst between your eyes and focus on your third eye opening up. Envision it inside your head getting stronger, power radiating from its core. Place the amethyst in front of you and meditate for as long as you can, I try to meditate for at least ten minutes at a time.

Do this ritual regularly and over time you will develop the ability of second sight as your third eye opens. It's possible to see a difference immediately after one ritual, but not common. Great power comes with practice and study! Your second sight is similar to a muscle in that your abilities of clairvoyance will grow with usage.

Ritual of Undoing

When a spell doesn't go as desired, whether it be a lack of focus, misdirected intention, or unexpected outcomes, it's good to perform a ritual of undoing to prevent any further harm. Think of it as sending energies out to negate the ones you wish to undo.

You will need:
Isa Rune
Paintbrush/paint or pen
Parchment/paper

"Isa Rune"

Isa is the Futhark rune of ice and represents binding, freezing cold and is the opposite of Fehu, the rune of movement. We'll be using Isa to freeze and negate those energies from the spell you wish to undo. Place your parchment in front of you and draw a large pentacle with your paint or pen, inside the pentacle draw the Isa rune. While thinking of the spell you wish to undo say the following:

> *"Freezing winds come blowing thru,*
> *Chill these forces I wish to undo,*
> *Frozen in place, impotent now,*
> *Only released if I allow."*

Fold or roll the paper up and keep it somewhere safe, if you wish to undo the undoing simply destroy the parchment.

Red Magic

The following chapter contains love spells. Some call it grey magic, some red and some people consider it to be black magic as it might influence the will of others.

While it is possible to craft a love spell that affects the will of another it can have undesired consequences, such as misdirecting your intentions and affecting the wrong person, or the resulting relationship being volatile. It's generally considered safer to craft spells that work to attract love in general, a type of magnetism. A safe and effective method is to craft a spell that asks your deities to lead someone to you that has the attributes and qualities you desire in a mate.

That being said, the possibilities are endless when it comes to red magic. I ask that you consult with your god, goddess, or ancestors before attempting any spell that could have life-changing consequences.

Honey Jar

Honey jars are well known folk rituals that works to sweeten someone's attitude towards you, encouraging them to have a favorable opinion of you and/or another, depending on your petition paper. It can be used to get positive attention that could lead to a relationship, a promotion, inclusion in inheritance, or anything else you wish to manifest. This is a type of Hoodoo folk magic which is widely used and well-known for its effectiveness. It can be accomplished using simple household items.

You will need:

Sealable jar or bottle

Pink or red candle

Honey or sugar

Picture or something representing the target

Rose petals, lavender and/or vanilla bean (optional)

Petition paper

Anoint (rub) the candle with the honey or sugar (mixed with a bit of water). Light the candle and prepare your space while focusing on what you wish to manifest. On the petition paper write what you wish the outcome of the ritual to be. For example, "Zack will see my worth and give me the promotion." Be as specific as possible for specific goals. Alternatively, you can write a general statement such as "love me", it all depends on what you are trying to accomplish.

Place the items into the jar one at a time while focusing on your intention and direct those energies into each item as they go into the jar. Close the jar and place your candle on top of the jar. Let the candle wax melt down onto the lid to "seal" the spell. Alternatively, you can drip the candle wax onto the jar if your jar or bottle isn't heatproof.

Keep the jar in a safe place until you no longer wish for the effects of the jar to remain active. To end the spell, unseal the jar and dispose of or recycle the contents.

Love Bell

This ritual is a magnetism spell that well help drawn in potential romance. All you need for this spell is a bell and a window or doorway.

Hang your bell in an open window or doorway and say the following.

"Little bell of love,
I hang you to whisper my need for love on the breezes and winds.
Little bell of love,
Speak of my need for love to your brothers and sisters.
Little bell of love,

I ask you to speak softly and draw to me one deserving of my heart."

Ring the bell three times, it is "whispering" of your need for love. The brothers and sisters are other bells who will add their own power to the spell as your bell rings out through the aether. Open your window or door and ring your bell three times every day until you find your love.

Candle Carving Ritual

In this spell you'll be using the power of the Wunjo rune to ask the gods to send you a companion.

You will need:
White candle
Carving tool
Altar

"Wunjo Rune"

Carve the Futhark Rune of Wunjo into the candle. Light the candle and say the following.

> *"I am strong, but incomplete,*
> *I ask the gods for no small feat.*
> *Send me love that's whole and pure,*
> *These lonely nights I can't endure.*
> *Joy and companionship are what I seek,*
> *Bring forth the one that is meant for me."*

Allow the candle to burn until it has reached the top of the rune carving and blow it out. Keep the candle on your altar until you've found the person you're looking for.

Aphrodite Sea Charm

This is a spell that utilizes the power of Aphrodite, the element of water, and the sea to enchant an item with the magnetism to attract a partner.

What you will need:
Seashell or other item representing the sea.
Small bag or container
Sea water

Place the shell on your altar. Splash some of your sea water onto the shell and say the following:

"Aphrodite, most beautiful goddess,
I ask you to bless this item with the charm and magnetism of your grace.
Give it the power to pull in someone worthy of my love and affection.
I give my eternal gratitude, blessed be!"

Place your shell in a small bag or container and take it with you when you're going to be around potential love interests.

Adoration Candle Spell

This weeklong ritual is a powerful spell that can bring two people closer together with the intent of starting a relationship.

You will need:
2 red candles
Rose oil

On a Friday night, the day of the week devoted to the Goddess Freya and Aphrodite, rub two red candles with rose oil. Place these candles on opposing ends of your altar. You may invoke either Freya or Aphrodite for your incantation. Light the candles and say the following:

"Freya!
Great goddess of love and the passions of man!
I set out on a path of love, romance, and adventure!
I seek adoration and endless possibilities!
If it be your will, bless this endeavor!
I ask you to bring us closer together!"

Every day for one week, with the last night being the next Friday, light the candles and move them slightly closer together. As you do this, imagine you and your love's energies coming closer together, and then blow out the candles.

On the seventh night, make sure the candles are as close as they can possibly be and light them. Meditate on your love and imagine the moment that you confess your love for one another. Let the candles burn all the way out.

Keep the wax from the candles and store it in a safe place. Dispose of the wax like in previous spells to break the magic of this ritual.

Hathor's Bath Ritual

This is a bathing ritual that is designed to draw a variety of people to you. The attraction bath calls upon the Egyptian Goddess Hathor, daughter of Ra and sky goddess of love, beauty, music, dance and joy. This spell will give you the confidence you need to get out there and let go, while highlighting your inner beauty.

You will need:
Red candles
Your favorite bathing oils
Rose petals
Mirror

Light the candles and add the rose petals and oils to your bath. Soak in the bath as long as you want. When you get out of the bath, dry off and stand in front of your mirror while reciting the following:

"I call on the blessings of Hathor, – Allow my inner beauty to shine through!
Make me an irresistible and joyous person,
So mote it be."

Give praise to Hathor as you gaze at yourself in the mirror. Picture an aura around your body that causes people to turn their heads and look at you. To nullify this spell, repeat the entire ritual word for word but with white candles.

Attraction Poppet

A spell utilizing a poppet/doll that targets a specific person that you're interested in. Freya is the Norse goddess of love and sorcery and we'll be asking her to bless our poppet, but you can use any deity you wish.

You will need:
Rose quartz crystal
Poppet
Target's picture
A pink cloth
Small box
Marker or paint
Raidho rune

Concentrate on your target being drawn towards you and see the relationship you will have once you magic has taken effect.

Draw the Raidho rune, which is the rune of motion and journeys, onto the picture while continuing to focus your intention.

Place your crystal on top of the picture and say the following:

"Noble Freya! I seek a love that outlasts all hardships, even death itself. Bless this doll with the magnetism to draw them in. If it be your will then bless this union. Blessed be!"

Take the pink cloth and sign your name on it. Wrap everything with the cloth and place it all in the box. Put the box in a safe place where it will not be disturbed. To cancel the spell, simply take the doll and cleanse it with sage smoke.

Love Knot

This witch's knot-style love spell will draw your true love to you. This doesn't compel the person to love you, it just gives you the opportunities you need to show them what you've got!

What you will need:
3 cords of varying colors

Take three cords or strings of various pleasing colors that make you think of love and passion, such as pink, red, and purple. Braid them tightly together while thinking of your heart's desire.

Firmly tie a knot in the middle of the braid while thinking of your need for love. Next, tie another knot, and another, until you have tied seven knots. Wear or carry the cord with you until you find your love.

Birch Bark Love Spell

This spell will utilize two strips of birch bark: one to initiate the spell and another to cast a sort of magical net from where you did the ritual to where you'll place the other piece.

You will need:
2 strips of birch bark
Red ink or paint
Cauldron
Bonfire/fireplace

Write the words "True Love" on a piece of the bark. Light your incense and throw the strip into the fire and say the following:

"Goddess of love, God of desire,
Bring to me, sweet passion's fire.
Love that's willing, love that's true,
This is all I ask of you."

Write the name of your preferred god or goddess on the second piece of bark and take it somewhere far away from where you burned the first piece. Ideally you want the second piece to be far enough away so that there's a lot of people residing in the area between the two pieces.

When you get to your second location say the following:

"Message of love, I set you free,
To find the one and return to me."

Place the bark on the ground and leave it there, concluding the ritual. To end the magnetic properties of this spell pour a cup of saltwater around the area that the first piece was burnt with the intentions of negating the spell.

Reverse Love Spell (Undoing)

This ritual will reverse any general love spell, whether it was cast on you or you cast it on someone else.

You will need:
Cup of rose petals
Half cup of mandrake or carrots
Sealable bottle
Bonfire or fireplace

Start a fire on a night when the moon is at its highest point. Take your mandrake and rose petals and throw them into the fire while saying the following:

"I call to the storms, I call to the breeze,
To scourge the ground and bend the trees,
I call upon you Hecate, to take this lover far away.
May they find love, true and pure,
But with them I can't endure."

After the fire burns out, take some of the ashes and put them in the bottle or container and then bury it to conclude the ritual.

A Seduction Spell

This is a three night long ritual that is sure to get the attention of anyone you wish. It works by targeting a specific person with large amounts of energy over the course of three nights.

You will need:
A red candle
Piece of red or pink paper
Pencil, pen, or paint
Cauldron

Light the red candle. Write your full name on the paper. Under your name, write the name of the person you're targeting, their birthday, and then your own.

Draw a heart around the information, then write the names again directly on top of the heart three times. Fold the paper in half and place it in your cauldron, light it with the candle. As it burns say the following:

"Light the flame bright, the fire is the color of desire.
Desire that manifests into a path of my choosing.
The desire I have I share with you,
Come to me and see all that I wish to show."

This must be done each night for three consecutive nights. This is a targeted ritual involving large amounts of your will, intention, and proper direction, so expect strong results if done successfully and a possible energy drain.

Aphrodisiac Potion

This potion will bring passion into the hearts of anyone who drinks it, whether it be you, your partner, or both. If you're wanting to spice things up with your significant other perform this ritual together and watch the sparks fly!

You will need:
Cauldron/pot for boiling
Saffron herb
Red candle
Honey
Chalice

Light the candle and bring one quart of water to a boil in your cauldron.

Add three pinches of saffron and remove from the heat. Cover the cauldron and allow the potion to steep for ten minutes. Strain out the saffron and pour one cup of the potion into your chalice. Add three teaspoons of honey and stir until mixed. Drink half of the potion and have your partner drink the other half. Blow out the candle together to conclude the ritual.

Aphrodisiac Bath

This aphrodisiac bath will make you irresistible to anyone you think about while bathing in it.

You will need:

3 parts rose petals

2 parts rosemary

1 part thyme

1 part saffron

1 part jasmine flowers

1 part acacia flowers

Put these ingredients into a pouch or just throw them in the tub and soak. Your partner will find you irresistible and you will smell great!

Passion Tea

This ritual works to stoke the flames of passion in yourself and anyone envisioned while imbibing.

You will need:

Red, pink, and green candle

6 cups water

4 caraway seeds

4 fennel seeds

1 teaspoon dried rosehip

Pinch of organic rose petals

Cauldron or pan for boiling the water

Tea diffuser (option)

Light the candles. Bring the water to a slow simmer and add your ingredients. Remove from heat and allow to steep for 10 minutes. While the tea steeps, concentrate on feelings of love. If you didn't use a diffusor, strain your tea and pour a cup. Find a comfortable, peaceful place to sit and drink your tea. If you have a picture of your intended target place it where you can look at it, otherwise you can simply visualize their face. If you wish for the spell to only affect you then simply think of yourself and the things you are passionate about. After you've drank the tea you can blow out the candles to conclude the ritual.

Black Magic

While there isn't a concrete color assignment to certain spells, per say, practitioners will typically refer to a spell as black or dark if the castor is influencing another's will or harming someone. Some refuse to work with any magic that does this because they believe the force will come back threefold. I have never experienced this blowback and any evidence I've seen of it has been anecdotal. The belief is rooted in an early 1900's practice called Gardnerian Wicca. If you're interested in learning more about the history of Wicca and witchcraft in general, check out my book *The Craft: Beginners Book of Witchcraft.*

While that is my experience, I won't deny that if you go beyond your limits there can be dire consequences. Exhaustion is common due to the high emotional energies needed for manifestation, but I've never heard of anyone dying as a direct result. I've come to believe that any negative consequences are likely due to improper direction of your intentions so instead of casting towards your intended target, the energy remains with the caster or an unintended target. This means the maladies caused by the spell affect them until cleansed. It's imperative that you maintain precise focus during manifestation. Your ritual tools, circle, gods/goddesses, and the ritual itself can assist you in properly setting and maintaining your intention.

For these reasons black magic spells can be potentially dangerous for the inexperienced and you should always cast a protection spell and a circle. If something goes wrong, take a salt-water bath, smudge cleanse or shower and clean yourself with a salt scrub while asking your deity for protection against whatever forces you've brought upon yourself. If you think your spell might have negatively affected another person that you didn't intend it's important to do a Ritual of Undoing which can also be found in this book.

Whatever your views on "Black Magic" might be I think that context is more important than anything. In my opinion curses, hexes and other forms of ensorcellment are simply tools, tools that can be used for good or evil and that is a matter of subjective opinion. I think it's important to learn about all kinds of magic, whether you think you might use them or not, knowledge is power and a powerful witch is a witch that's prepared for anything with all available tools at their disposal.

Shadow Circle

A shadow circle is a sacred and shielded place to conduct rituals that require the utmost concentration and focus, especially useful when conducting malevolent rituals. Cast this circle to prevent any stray energies that could potentially interrupt or hinder your ability to concentrate and focus your intentions. The circle is actually a sphere of protection that can potentially be any size that you wish. In this ritual I'll be using an athame to cast the circle, but you could use a wand, your hand, or a staff. Pretty much any phallic tool will work.

You will need:
Athame, wand, staff, or hand
Space to create a circle

Visualize the darkness flowing around you. Take your athame in your left hand and thrust it southwards, in a counterclockwise motion, then turn 360 degrees until you arrive back at the southern starting point.

As the shadows circle around you, feel the pressure build and the shadow energy compressing against you. Feel the cold of the abyss all around you: feel it's chill, but don't let it affect your concentration.

As the shadows close in, push them back into a six-foot circle around you, creating a barrier of darkness. This is your shadow circle, a protected sacred place that will allow you to conduct your rituals uninterrupted.

Now you may conduct a ritual, meditate, or anything else that requires perfect focus. Close the circle by cutting it with your athame in your dominant hand. Spend time meditating inside the shadow circle to strengthen your concentration, power, and ability to focus your intentions when conducting potentially harmful magic.

Invocation of Lyssa, Goddess of Rage

Rage and anger are a key element in a lot of black magic rituals, and the Goddess of Rage is known to many as Lyssa. It's a good idea to familiarize yourself with her and ask for her help when conducting these types of spells. The following is a pact ritual to ask her to aid you in the building of rage.

To call upon Lyssa make three pentacles on the ground. Position them as if they are forming the points of a triangle and make sure they're far enough apart so you can stand in the center. You may construct your pentacles in any way. Concentrate on all the things you hate, and when you have built up a rage call out to the goddess Lyssa with the following prayer.

"Oh, Great Goddess Lyssa,
Daughter of the Noble Nyx.
I ask for your assistance and guidance,
I, like you, are a child of the darkness,
I foster rage in my heart,
Aid me in releasing it upon my enemies,
I wish to be your disciple,
teach me the art of rage,
guide me in my endeavors,
together we can accomplish anything,

grant me the power to destroy."

If you feel her presence you have succeeded in connecting with Lyssa. If you don't, then you need to meditate on your inner rage and try again. A pact with Lyssa is a great boon to practitioners of the dark arts and is worth practicing as there aren't any potential negative effects or intention that could be inadvertently directed.

I can't stress how helpful it is to have a connection with a divine being of some sort as can it really aid in properly directing your intentions during rituals, this can also be accomplished through animist connections to nature if you aren't interested in working with the gods. Pray to and make offerings to Lyssa on a regular basis to keep her favor.

Sour Jar

Sour jars work to sour the life of your target. This Hoodoo folk magic can be used to target a single person but are often used to break up a relationship, be it romantic, familial or even job-related. Sour jars can be made in a number of ways but typically contain a sour/acidic liquid, such as vinegar, as the base and other intention-charged items to represent and focus the energies being used in the curse. Like other jar spells, this ritual can be customized to fit your needs with the important thing being your intention and focus during the process of crafting the jar. The following is a traditional Hoodoo sour jar ritual.

> You will need:
> Jar or bottle with metal lid
> Any type of vinegar
> Nails
> Hot sauce or peppers
> Pepper flakes/powder
> Picture or something representing the targets
> Petition paper
> Black candle

Envision what you want to achieve from this ritual and keep that in your mind throughout the entire ritual. Anoint (rub) the candle with some of the vinegar, sprinkle some of the pepper flakes onto the candle and light it.

Pour the vinegar into the jar until it's about half full. On your petition paper, write what you wish to occur. It can be as simple as writing, "soured life" or detailed as, "their relationship will sour and lead to separation". Place your items in one at a time while focusing your intention. Close the jar and place the candle on top of the jar. Let the wax run down onto the lid, "sealing" the jar. If your jar isn't metal or heatproof, you can drip the wax onto the jar to seal it.

Every day for seven days, give the jar a shake while refocusing your intentions. Be careful if using raw vinegar or other organic matter as pressure might build inside the jar, causing it to burst, especially if the jar is being kept in a warm place. Alternatively, you could relight the candle each day to refocus your intentions and reinvigorate the energies of the spell. After seven days you may dispose of the jar in any way you see fit.

Effigy Poppet Curse

You will need:
Effigy or poppit
Black candle
Fireproof container

The effigy curse utilizes an image or representation (effigy) of the intended victim and the flame of a black candle. The effigy can be anything you wish. Their name on a small piece of paper is pragmatic and simple. Keep in mind you're about to set the effigy on fire.

The amount of damage done to the victim is correlated with the amount of energy and rage you put into the ritual. This ritual will typically cause misfortune in the form of injury or the loss of something they hold dear. Advanced practitioners can direct their intentions to achieve a specific outcome.

Light the black candle on your altar and place a fireproof bowl or plate in front of the candle. Carefully take your effigy and set the corner on fire using the candle, do this in a well-ventilated space, preferably outside. Immediately drop the effigy in the bowl and chant the following aloud.

> *"This is the time of retribution,*
> *I invoke the elements,*
> *I summon them,*
> *I conjure them to do my bidding,*
> *The four watchtowers, grant me thy power,*
> *Bring forth fear, guilt and pain,*
> *There shall be submission without pity,*
> *I direct my hate against thee,*
> *Against thee it shall be directed,*
> *A hundred-fold is the cost for my anger and pain,*
> *Thee shall be wrought with fear, anointed with pain,*
> *Blinded by me, binded by me, cursed by me, So mote it be!"*

Once the fire has burnt out you may extinguish the candle to conclude the ritual.

Ring of Power Enchantment

Many practitioners of the dark arts will enchant different objects to strengthen a bond with a deity or to increase one's dark energies. One of the most common items to be imbued with this power is a ring. In this enchantment we will be asking Lyssa, The Goddess of Rage, to imbue our ring with her blessing.

You will need:
A ring
Bowl of offerings
Two black candles
One red candle

Start off by placing a small bowl with nuts and/or fruits on your altar as an offering to the Goddess. Light two black candles and place them on opposite sides of your altar. Place a red candle in between the black candles and place your ring at the base of the red candle in a way so that the wax will drip down onto the ring.

Concentrate on the anger and hatred for anything you may have and let that anger build up until you have worked yourself up into a rage.

Say the following:

"Lyssa, Great Lyssa, I ask that you grant me a boon of strength.

This ring before you is mine and now yours.

When I wear it, I may call upon your power and you may call upon my service.

Goddess of Madness and Rage come forth and be bound to me through mutual fury and hatred,

I will not waste your strength, my goddess."

Extinguish the black candles and let the red candle burn until the wax touches the ring. This is when the enchantment is complete.

Remove the ring from the altar and put it on. If successful you should feel the power coursing through your body. If not, I suggest working on your connection with the goddess and your own inner rage.

You may wear the ring in any way: on a necklace, in your pocket, in a bag, etc.

As long as you retain your bond with Lyssa and give her regular offerings and prayers your ring should maintain its power.

Nightmare Jar

This jar spell will bring the target severe nightmares.

You will need:
Item representing the target
Sand
Poppy seeds
Valerian root or powder
Vinegar
Something to seal the jar

Focus on your target and the nightmares they'll have as you pour in the sand until it's about half an inch deep. Place your item representing the target on top of the sand. Pour your poppy seeds and valerian in while maintaining your intention, and then pour the vinegar in until it's about halfway full.

Close the jar and seal it with candle wax, glue, ribbon, string or whatever you have on hand.

Shake the jar every night you want the target to have nightmares, when you are finished with the jar you may dispose of it in with any method you wish.

Stone of Sorrow

You can use this ritual to siphon the joyous energy from a person who has wronged you into a stone which you may discard or use for other purposes.

You will need:
Small stone
Clear view of the moon

While outside at night grip the stone loosely. Envision the person who you wish to inflict this punishment upon. Feel your grip tightening as your anger builds. When you feel that you've reached the peak of your rage say the word "Release!" out loud, envision the joy exploding out of their body and see all the energy coming towards you and into the stone in your hand.

When all the energy has been trapped inside the stone, throw it in the opposite direction from the moon or keep the stone for later usage. The more powerful in the dark arts you are the more joy you'll be able to remove from their soul. Do this ritual sparingly and only when absolutely necessary because it can be taxing on your own stores of energy. To undo the spell you can either break the stone or conduct a Ritual of Undoing.

Stone of Jinxing

This is a variation I created of the last spell but it works on their luck. Do the same ritual but before getting rid of the stone say the following.

"I don't caste away this stone, but the wellbeing and fortune of (Name), so that their prosperity should flow away like the coursing water and their endeavors may never bear fruit again!"

Unceremoniously discard the stone.

Poppet Curse of Slight Pain

Not every wrong deserves a broken leg or the flu, so try this poppet spell out instead. A poppet can be any sort of doll that you can use to focus your intentions and direct the forces being used upon the unsuspecting. Your poppet can be anything from a hand-sewn doll to a soap carving.

You will need:
Poppet (effigy doll)

Take your poppet and hold it in your dominant hand. Think of your victim as you slowly tighten your grip around the poppet. When you reach the level of malevolence you wish to imbue into the doll, release the poppet and let it fall to the floor.

Pick up the poppet. It is now ready to be used to harm your target.

You can do anything to this poppet from thumping it on the leg to cause a slight bruise to sneezing on it with the intentions of giving them a cold. The damage you'll be able to do with poppet magic is directly related to your ability in the dark arts and the amount of rage you instilled into the poppet while thinking of your victim. You may add candles and incense to this ritual to increase its power. You will improve the potency of all your spells as you continue down your path, but this is a great starting point for anyone interested in the dark arts.

Binding by Fear

This ritual works to prevent an assailant from causing you harm and can prevent them from being able to curse, hex or bewitch you in any way, binding them with fear. When they start their incantations, they will be gripped by terror and cease their malevolence.

You will need:
Effigy or poppet
Fairly long thread or cord

Attach the effigy (image/representation) of the person to the thread, you can tie the thread around effigy or attach it with wax, glue or any other binding agent. After you've attached effigy say the following:

"This is the effigy of my would-be assailant.
I hang it from a single thread in a place only known by me.
It will bring fear in the heart of my aggressor.
He will be binded from his abilities.
His power is nothing against mine.
The knot I create shall bind his will.
Until it breaks,
So mote it be."

Tie a knot in the thread to conclude the spell.

You may bury or hide the effigy away anywhere you like, you could also keep the effigy in a freezer to fully bind the target from all magical workings. You may undo this ritual by breaking the connection of the knot and the effigy, you can simply cut the cord between the two or destroy the whole thing in a bonfire.

Evil Eye Enchantment

The evil eye is an ancient ability that has been known to nearly every culture throughout the world. This ritual will imbue the power of the evil eye into a ring so that you may invoke its destructive powers whenever you wish.

You will need:
Ash (incense ash/wood ash)
Ring
Paper
Black candle

Draw the Isa rune on your paper with the ash. Place the ring on the paper and light the black candle. Say the following:

"Atë, daughter of Eris, Queen of evil and ruin.
Share with me your gift, so that I may aid in your never-ending quest of destruction!"

Hold the ring in the air with your dominant hand and blow out the candle.

By simply wearing this ring and looking at a person while focusing your intention, you can bring them misery and misfortune. Be careful with its use as you've created a powerful artifact that has been blessed by the goddess Atë with powers of ruin and chaos. Only wear this ring when you wish to cast the evil eye to prevent accidental casting of intentions.

Bones of Anger

This hex will instill depression and anger into the heart of the victim.

You will need:
Bell
Dried chicken bones

When you are ready to cast this curse work yourself into a rage. As stated before, this will add to the potency of the spell. During the casting of the spell when it says, *"with these bones I now do crush",* use your feet to grind the bones into the ground as if they were your enemy.

Ring the bell 3 times and say the following:

"Lyssa, Lady of Fury! Lend me your rage so we may crush my opposition!"

When you feel Lyssa's presence continue with the spell.

"Bones of fury, turn to dust,
Full of anger, revenge is just.
I crush these bones, these bones of rage,
Take my enemy, bring them pain.
I see my enemy before me now.
I bind them, destroy them, cast them down.
With these bones that I do crush.
Make my enemy turn to dust,
Torment, anguish, out of control,
With this hex I curse their soul.
So mote it be!"

Succubae's Lament (Dream Invasion)

Succubae are spirits that invade a person's dreams. They are mischievous, chaotic entities which makes them prime candidates for exploitation through dark ritual.

To influence a succubus, you need to have your intentions very clear in your mind. You could send a succubus construct any kind of dream, and what they do will be determined by your intentions and the "song" you sing to them.

It's best to write your own song and tailor it to your needs but here's one that will work for most occasions:

"Succubae, Succubae,
hear my song and hear my cries.
The one I love is so far away,
but in his thoughts, I wish to stay.
Seek him high and seek him low,
fill his dreams with passion, go!."

After singing this, lay in bed and concentrate on exactly how you want the dream to go.

Succubae aren't commonly called upon by humans and they will likely be more than pleased to help you with your invasive dream-scaping.

Summon a Storm

You will need:
Altar
Blue candle
Chalice of water

You don't need an ocarina to summon a storm, you can do it with magic! Weather working is considered by some to be a dark art as its consequences can affect others negatively. For example, you could create a rainstorm and inadvertently cause someone to wreck and if you harbor enmity and rage towards a person they could be struck by lightning if they're in range of the storm.

If you're creating a storm without the intention of harming anyone it's very important to clear your mind of all anger towards anyone. If your intention is to use the storm to harm someone then focus on the person you wish the storm to harm. Keep in mind that controlling a storm once summoned is extremely difficult and should only be attempted if you're very confident in your ability.

Light a blue candle upon your altar and meditate on your intentions and the desired location of the storm. While staring into the light of the candle, chant the following:

"I call upon the winds of the North,
Awake from your slumber,
Drain the waters from the earth and bring them down in sheets of agony."

Toss the water from the chalice into the air so that it falls onto the earth, if your doing this ritual indoors you can toss the water out a window. Blow out your candle to conclude the ritual.

Three Nights of Hell

You will need:
Effigy
Black candle
Altar

This is a classic spell that I've adapted to torment a person with pain for three nights. It rarely ends in serious injury and is typically used to warn your enemies and display your power.

Light the candle on your altar and tilt it at an angle so that the wax will drip on the effigy. As the wax drips, envision it causing sores and pain to your victim. While doing this, say the following:

> *"As I cast this darkened spell*
> *Bring my enemy three nights of hell*
> *Candle black, black as night*
> *Bring them pain and bring them fright!*
> *Lesions on their body grow*
> *Afflict them with a hateful blow*
> *Sores and pain consume them now*
> *For three nights they won't know how*
> *Kings of darkness, dukes of hell*
> *Crush my enemy, time will tell*
> *When three nights have come to pass*

Make him well, well at last".

Spend a moment in silence envisioning malevolent forcing coming down upon your enemy, after you've done this blow out the candle to conclude the ritual.

A Seduction Spell

You will need:
A red candle
Piece of red or pink paper
Red ink pen

Light the red candle. On the paper write your full name. Under your name, write the name of the person you desire, their birthday, and then your own.

Draw a heart around the information and then write the names and birthdays again directly on top of the heart. Do this three times. Don't worry if it looks like scribble. Fold the paper small and burn it in the flame of the candle. As it burns say the following three times:

"Light the flame bright, the fire red is the color of desire. "

Blow out the candle to conclude the ritual, repeat this ritual for the following 2 nights for a total of three times.

Severed Love

This powerful marriage hex will bring chaos and strife into the relationship of a couple. Though traditionally the intention of the spell is to ruin a marriage this ritual can affect any sort of relationship.

You will need:
4 black candles
Picture of victims
Oil
Red marker
Hammer and nails
Block of wood

Anoint the candles with the oil while setting your intention. Visualize the destruction that you intend to cause, the more time you meditate on this the more powerful the hex will be.

Draw a heart on the chest and head of a person in the picture and place it on the block of wood. Drive a nail through the chest and say the following:

*"With this nail I pierce your heart
soon your love will surely part."*

Do the same thing but this time driving the nail through the head and say:

*"With this nail I pierce your mind
insanity you'll surely find."*

Place the black candles around the picture, corresponding to north, south, east and west. Make sure the wax from the candles can drip onto the picture. Light the candles and meditate on all the negative things that will be assailing the couple while the wax drips down onto the picture. When you feel that you have instilled enough hateful power into this spell recite the following:

*"Lords of Darkness, Demons of the Night
Bring this hex into full flight.
End the Bond before me now,
Bring its destruction, bring them down.
Take their marriage and break it apart,
Bring them chaos, pierce their hearts.
Shred their love to pieces so fine,
What's there is gone, now is the time.
Never again shall they be together,*

Their happiness shall now be severed.
When their love, it starts to smother,
Each will want to end the other.
No longer shall they be as one,
Your marriage is over, what's done is done!
Lords of Darkness, Demons of the Night,
Bring this Curse, now to flight!"

When you dispose of the things used in this spell make it as unceremonious and worthless as the relationship you have destroyed.

Discord and Darkness

This knot curse will bring chaos into the life of someone who has wronged you. Nothing will seem to go right for them and they will fall into a great despair.

You will need:
Long piece of yarn

You'll need a piece of yarn (or any thick string or rope) at least ten inches long. Recite the following three parts and tie a knot as you say each one.

First knot:
> *"With this knot I seal this hex,*
> *You shall not sleep, you shall not rest.*
> *Knot of strife, knot of hate,*
> *Discord brings you this dark fate "*

Second knot:
> *"This knot I tie, now makes two,*
> *Bringing anguish over you,*
> *Sadness, loss and evil too.*
> *Bringing darkness straight and true. "*

Third knot:
> *"With the third, I do bind,*
> *Breeding chaos in your mind,*
> *Hex of anger, hex of hate,*
> *Crashing down, I cannot wait"*

As you conduct this ritual it is imperative to maintain your focus and direct your rage properly. If you decide to break this hex, burn the string with the flame of a white candle.

Tattered Hearts Part 1

This is a ritual that can be done in two parts, the first part is to dissolve the relationship of a couple and the second is to attract one of the targets of the first ritual.

You will need:
2 hearts cut out of cloth
Needle and thread
Marker/paint
Red and black candle

Write the names of the couple, one on each heart. Sew the hearts together - a few stiches will do. Light the candles and say the following:

> *"What has been drawn together,*
> *Can soon be torn apart,*
> *The stars align, but fade with time,*
> *And then you will depart."*

Tear the hearts apart and blow out the candle.

Tattered Hearts Part 2

Take the damaged heart of the person you want to attract and place it in a bowl of sea water and say the following:

"I know you might feel broken,
I've come to mend your heart,
With darkness fled, until your dead,
I'll always do my part."

Remove the heart and place it somewhere safe to dry. This spell will stay in effect until the heart is cleansed and destroyed. To do this, burn the heart with the flame of a white candle.

Doll of Pain

You will need:
3 Black candles
Poppet (doll)
Pins/knives

This is my take on a classic black magic ritual. The poppet and pins are used while utilizing your anger and hatred to make a connection to the target, delivering immediate and intense pain.

Light three black candles on your alter as you work up a rage. Take a poppet that represents your victim and pierce it with a pin or knife as you imagine pain coursing through the person's body. While piercing the doll, recite the following:

"Smitten, beaten, battered and torn,
I stab at thee with all my scorn
Suffer now I cannot wait
With this I will seal your fate
Pins so sharp and made of steel
I strike at thee, this mark you'll feel
Smitten, beaten, battered and torn
I curse you now, your pain is born!"

Remove the pins from the doll and extinguish the candles to conclude the ritual. You can keep the doll to cleanse and reuse, bury it in the ground, or stick it in the freezer to keep the target from striking back at you.

Carman's Hex

I once met a wise old Irish woman who told me of this casual hex she knew that I quickly scrawled down into my Book of Shadows, it's beautiful in its simplicity.

"Chairs, tables, knives, forks,
Tankards, bottles, cups and corks,
Dishes, beds, boots and keg,
Bacon, pudding, milk and egg,
Every pillow, sheet and bed
The dough in the trough, and the baked bread,
Every bit of provender on the shelf, and all you will have left is the house itself!"

Vanity and Insanity

This is a spell crafted with the vain in mind. Upon successful casting of this spell, the victim will be overwhelmed with a sense of abominable ugliness. When they look in the mirror, they'll find they no longer love the image they're seeing, and their flaws will forever be highlighted in their minds and hearts.

You will Need:
Something from the victim
Flammable effigy
Fireproof cauldron
Black candle
Black marker or paint

Take something belonging to the victim, like hair, nail clipping or even a pencil belonging to them would work, if you can't acquire anything like this you could use a picture of them. Write the words "Self-Love" on the effigy with a black marker or paint. Place all of this in a fire-proof cauldron in a well-ventilated area and use a black candle to set the effigy on fire. As the fire burns recite the following:

> *"(Persons name) who now I see,*
> *will go insane from vanity.*
> *They'll see themselves as others do,*
> *all good looks are gone from you.*
> *What was is not and now it's true,*
> *all your beauty flees from you.*
> *You look in the mirror, yourself to tend,*
> *your conjured beauty has come to an end.*
> *Your awful ego is now broken,*
> *you'll go insane in that same token.*
> *I take this all away from you,*

because of all the things you do.
Once you thought you were so great,
I bring you down to meet your fate.
In your mind you'll go insane, vanity is now your pain."

Take some of the ashes from the cauldron and spread them in the vicinity of the victim, alternatively you can go outside and toss the ashes in their direction.

Pepper Pentacle

This is a simple bad luck spell utilizing the power of the pentacle and pepper. Your victim will experience bad luck until the spell is undone.

You will need:
Paper
Pen
Black pepper
Black candle

Draw a pentacle (pictured above) on the paper and write the victim's name in the middle. Sprinkle pepper around the outside of the pentacle.

Light your candle and hold it over the pentacle. Let the wax drip down until the persons entire name is covered. If you wish to undo this curse you may burn the paper in the flames of a white candle.

Bad Luck Potion

You will need:
1 cup of water
Cauldron
Salt
Sealable jar/container
Dead flower

Add about a cup of water to the cauldron and set it on the fire to boil. Once boiling, add the flower and the salt. Recite the following:

> *"This water boiling, full of hate.*
> *Brings bad luck at alarming rates."*

Watch the water boil and feel your own anger bubbling inside of you. Direct that energy into your water, stir the water clockwise 9 times and allow the pot to boil for about 3 minutes. Allow the water to cool down a bit, strain the contents of the potion and pour the water into your bottle. Seal up the bottle. Repeat the words of the spell again, say the name of your victim aloud and seal the bottle to conclude the ritual.

Take the potion and put it somewhere safe and out of sight or bury it. Open the container and spill the contents to reverse the curse.

Forbidden Death Curse

Most dark magic is intended to teach someone a lesson or to force your will upon another. In some extreme cases, the persons flame might need to be permanently extinguished. I ask you seek guidance from Hecate or your deity before making that decision. Be aware that this type of ritual is frowned upon by most practitioners as most wish to change their target's ways, not kill them, since this can have severe ripple effects and unintended consequences. While I strongly advise against resorting to this type of working I believe there are cases where a ritual like this might be justified, specifically in cases of abuse and coercion when other means have been exhausted.

You will need:
3 black candles
Chalice filled with moon water
Offerings

Light the candles and cast a circle, place the offerings upon your alter and work yourself up into a concentrated rage while focusing on the demise of your intended target.

Say the following:

"This person needs to be put to rest. I call upon the Dark Goddess to fulfill this wish!
This is the final chapter of (person's name) life, his/her story has come to an end!
Hecate! Send your Hounds!"

Extinguish the candles to conclude the ritual. For my ritual I invoke Hecate as I have a strong bond with her, this might differ for you so adjust the spell accordingly.

Sigil Magic

Sigils are symbols that are used as representations for a god, goddess, or other spiritual entity. They can also be created and charged by a practitioner to achieve a desired outcome. So, in a way, they are like spells in that we use them to accomplish our needs.

In medieval magic, sigils were used to represent various Angels and Demons and there were many magical training books for sigils, called grimoires. A well-known grimoire from this era, "The Lesser Key of Solomon", lists 72 sigils which correspond to 72 demons of hell. Sigils were considered to be a type of "true name" for these entities and gave the practitioner a measure of control over these magical beings. A common method of creating these sigils were to convert the names of the spirits into numbers and plot them on a magic square. The points would then be connected by lines to form an abstract symbol representing the entity to be used in ritual work to worship or invoke the spirit.

Witches today generally use sigils to create affirmations and to affect change in their lives by creating sigils that are charged with our intent. There are many methods to create sigils and it can really be anything that represents any sort of concept that you wish to manifest.

When doing sigil magic to manifest something, you generally start out with a statement of intent. Avoid negative statements such as "I will not be anxious" and opt for a positive statement such as "I am calm and confident". Here's a few examples of statements of intent.

"My family is healthy and strong"
"Self-confidence"
"I desire inner peace"
"I wish to honor the goddess"

For this example, we're going to use "My family is healthy and strong".

From this point, you simplify this statement as much as possible to create an abstract symbol that represents your desire.

Cross out any letters in the sentence that repeat. You may also cross out vowels (AEIOU) to further simplify the sentence. So, the letters you will be left with in this example are:

"MYFLSHTNDRG"

Now use all these letters to create a symbol that represents your desire: in this case, for your family to be healthy and strong. You can be as creative as you wish when creating your symbols. Your letters can be of differing sizes and can be flipped in any direction as you construct your sigil. There are other advanced methods to create sigils that involve plotting out the letters on a grid, usually circular, and then connecting the points to make your sigil. I'll be showing you the method which, in my opinion, is most beginner-friendly and holds just as much power as the more advanced methods.

Symbols can overlap to further simplify the sigil. For example, the following symbol can be used as a simplified version of the letters S Y V and L, each letter making up parts of other letters.

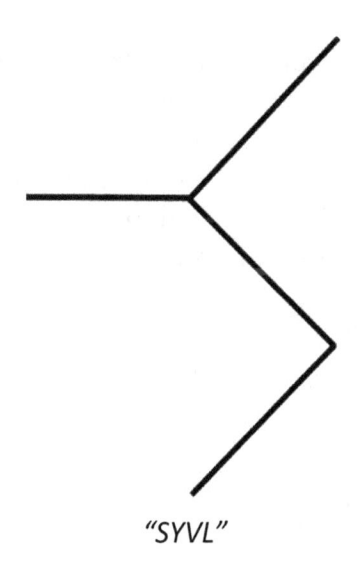

"SYVL"

You can use straight lines, curves, or abstract symbols to create your sigils. The important thing is that the symbol represents your intent.

Now, our statement of intent is, "my family is healthy and strong" and the letters we reduced it to are "MYFLSHTNDRG". Let's put them all together, see what we get and then go from there:

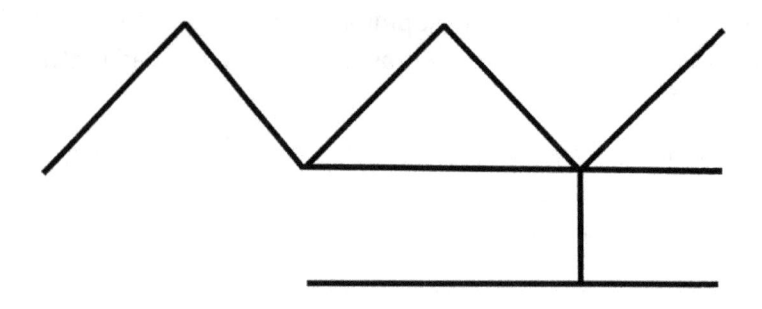

This symbol contains all the letter compiled into a single image. Now, from this point you can further simplify the symbol or continue with the creation of your sigil. I'd like to make my symbol a bit more simplified so that when I create the circle for the sigil everything is compact and fits nicely without being too wide or narrow. As you can see, I started with the M and added all the letters on from there. I'm going to further simplify it by taking the left half of my M and moving it over to the other side, to make a more ideal abstract symbol for my sigil.

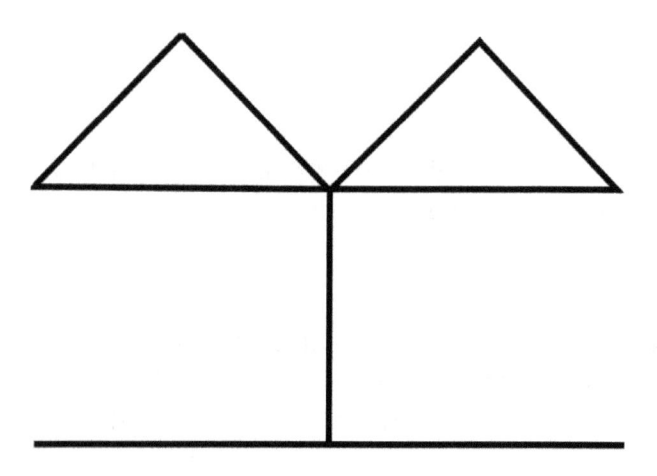

At this point you can draw a circle around your sigil or cut it out to create an area where the energies you transfer to the sigil will be contained.

Now it's time to activate your sigil. This step involves clearing your mind and focusing solely on your desires and channeling those desires into your sigil. There are a number of ways to charge the sigil: chanting, dance, song, orgasm, meditation. However, what you are essentially doing is focusing your intentions and energies and directing them into the sigil.

After your sigil has been charged and activated, you are free to do with it as you see fit. Many choose to destroy the sigil by tearing, burning, soaking, burying, or any other means of destruction. You can also do this by cutting or erasing the lines, releasing the energies of the sigil back into the cosmos.

In traditional Chaos Magick you "forget" the sigil at this point. By putting the sigil out of our minds, we allow it to work in our subconscious as a symbol representing the intention and the words we used to create it. This allows the sigil to do its work, undisturbed by our conscience minds bombardment of unintended intentions which might influence the workings of the sigil.

This is just a basic way to conduct sigil magic and there are many other methods that vary from practitioner to practitioner. You can get as creative as you like: there's no correct way to construct your sigils. The important thing is that you're creating a symbol that represents your intentions.

Divination

Divination is the process of using objects such as cards or runes to better understand our past, present, and future. We use these interpretive tools to connect us to the divine and the cosmos for understanding and guidance. Divination has been practiced by pagans, witches, and heathens for thousands of years and is one of the most ancient magics known to mankind. Like everything in witchcraft there are multiple methods to achieve the same goal so feel free to use whatever methods and tools you that you feel most connected to.

Some of the more common forms of divination use tarot cards, rune casting, spirit boards, bones, candle wax, and various forms of scrying. You might hear of water-, crystal ball-, smoke- or candle-gazing which are also forms of scrying. Any of these, or a number of other tools, can help you develop your intuition and give you insight into different aspects of your life and the lives of others with practice.

Divination takes much practice, and you will likely find that some methods work better for you than others. As you become more familiar with the practice you will strengthen your intuition, develop your spiritual-self, and become more skilled in the art of divination.

While most people might think of fortune-telling when they hear divination, the true power of divination lies in being able to see the forces that have, are, and will affect our past, present, and future so that we may adapt, grow, and change our current and future situations. Think of divination as a way of looking at the threads of fate and the forces that surround them.

For example, if you have a negative reading or sign pertaining to the future, don't get upset. The future is not set in stone and through divination we are able to see our current trajectory and course correct to achieve a better outcome. In contrast, good or positive signs let us know that we are currently on the right path to where we want to be. As you become more experienced, you will get better and better at interpreting the signs and what they mean regarding your life. Always make sure to meditate on the signs and think deeply on the information you are given and how it relates to your circumstances.

In the next section I'm going to be sharing my favorite method of divination, rune casting. Keep in mind that there are many different methods of divination, and you will likely find a way that you prefer as well as you continue down your path.

Rune Casting

Rune casting is a type of divination using runes, typically the Futhark Runes, to gain insight on our past, present, and future. The Futhark Runes are an ancient magical alphabet given to mankind by the god Odin. I'll go over the Futhark Runes and their meanings later in the book.

Rune casting is done in a similar way as Tarot. You select at random and place (cast) one, three, or more runes to get insight from the divine as it pertains to the past, present and future.

Three Norns Method

This simple beginner method is named after The Three Norns, who are Norse Goddesses and the weavers of fate. The diviner draws three runes from a bag or box and places them in front of them one at a time to reveal the past, present, future as it pertains to the situation in question. It is possible to do a general reading or ask about a specific situation.

The first rune placement is "The Place of Urd". The rune in this position reveals the past events that have a direct relation to the present situation and form the foundation of future events.

The second rune placement is "The Place of Verdandi". This rune refers to the current situation or choices that must be made in the very near future.

The third rune placement is "The Place of Skuld". This rune refers to the veiled future. This position can reveal an aspect of your future and can show where the path you are currently on will take you.

When doing any kind of divination, be preceptive to the divine. We are searching for their wisdom, and they are connecting to us and sharing their knowledge through the tools that we use during divination. Before casting, you might want to meditate on the information you wish to receive. Focus on the specific aspect of your life you're seeking guidance on. You may also wish to make an offering to your gods, goddesses, and ancestors and welcome their guidance as you look for the answers you seek.

Regardless of the method, take time after divination to meditate on the reading you receive. If you are confused, ask for clarity and be perceptive to signs you might receive. I like to keep a dream journal to record any insight I might get while dreaming because the barriers between our realm and the divine are thin in the dreamscape.

Scrying

Scrying is the practice of divining the future or seeking answers by gazing into a reflective surface such as a mirror, water, or a crystal ball.

Scrying is almost like dreaming with your eyes open. We allow ourselves to slip into a meditative state while gazing into any reflective surface. While in this receptive state, we can perceive signs that can be interpreted to get an idea of what the future may hold. Scrying takes a lot of practice and the more you learn about symbols and their meanings, the better you will become at accurately discerning what you're seeing.

When I'm scrying, I like to place a candle behind my crystal ball and gaze into the flame as it dances. I find it mesmerizing, and it helps me get into a meditative state quickly to perceive the signs my gods wish to show me. Find a way that works for you and practice, practice, practice! Scrying can be very therapeutic, will help you develop your intuition, and is a great entry level way to get into divination. While learning to scry can be easy, mastering it can take many years.

Pendulum Dowsing

Pendulum dowsing uses an object, usually a crystal that is attached to a string or chain. You then ask a question and hold the pendulum over a chart or graph. The direction the pendulum swings in reveals an answer.

The answer that the pendulum reveals isn't necessarily set in stone, because as we've learned already, fate is not set, and our course always has the potential to be changed.

Any type of chart can be used, you can even forgo the use of a chart and just designate cardinal directions as specific answers, such as north/south mean 'yes', and east/west mean 'no'.

This is just one of many ways for the divine to reveal hidden information and give guidance. Here are a few example charts that you might wish to duplicate and use for your own practice. You may also make your own!

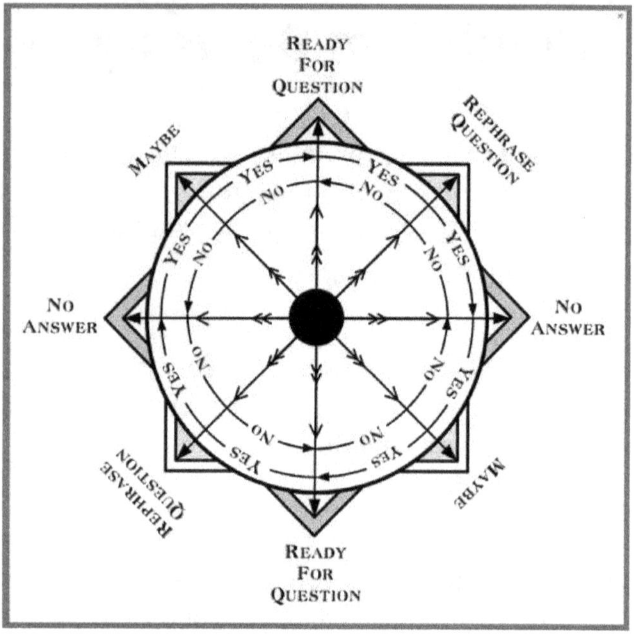
READY FOR QUESTION
REPHRASE QUESTION
MAYBE
YES
NO
NO ANSWER
NO ANSWER
MAYBE
REPHRASE QUESTION
READY FOR QUESTION

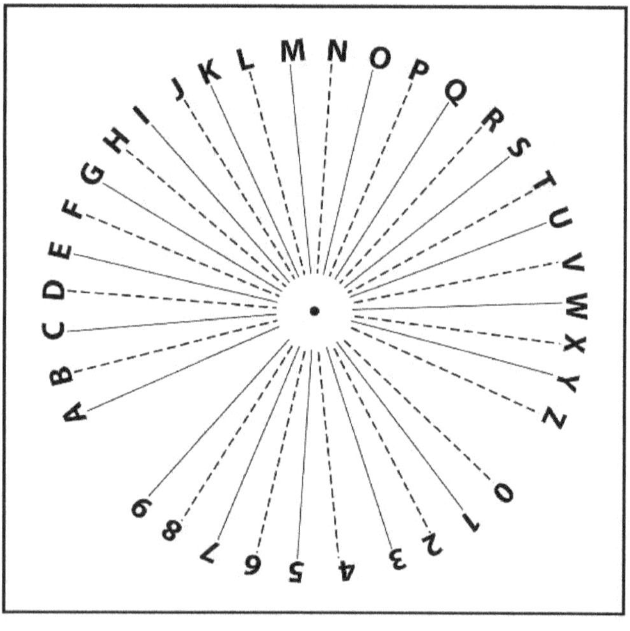
A B C D E F G H I J K L M N O P Q R S T U V W X Y Z
0 1 2 3 4 5 6 7 8 9

The Futhark Runes

The Futhark Runes have been especially important to my own path. I've always felt a close connection to these ancient symbols and the gods that granted them to mankind. I meditate on the runes frequently and include them in much of my ritual work. They're also my go to form of divination.

Norse legend says that the All-Father Odin hung from Yggdrasil, The World Tree, for nine days and nights, staring into the Well of Urd. He had pierced himself with his own spear to prove he was worthy of the knowledge that the Norns possessed. On the ninth night, the Runes revealed themselves to him and granted him all the knowledge they held. Odin's powers greatly multiplied, making him one of the most powerful entities in the cosmos.

These runes can be used in divination or be directly applied to anything to imbue the magical properties that the runes represent. They can also be used alongside any ritual to boost the powers and energies of the forces represented by the runes.

FEHU (Cattle)

Germanic: Fe (Fehu)
Gothic: Faihu
Norse: Fé
Anglo-Saxon: Feo, Feoh
Icelandic: Fé
Norwegian: Fe

Fehu literally translated means 'cattle'. It is a symbol of wealth, property and prosperity. This is the rune of luck and, as such, has the capacity to harbor luck and make use of it. Fehu has the power to bless new endeavors and assist in making new goals. While being a rune of wealth, the fact that it is also directly tied to luck suggests that an altruistic nature is required to make use of its power because luck is a result of courageous deeds. Fehu is a useful rune to use when performing rituals related to wealth, luck, love and prosperity.

Stones associated with this rune are tiger eye, carnelian, citrine, and aventurine.

ÜRUZ (AUROCHS)

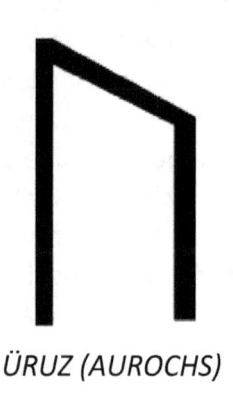

Anglo-Saxon: UR
Germanic: Uraz (Uruz)
Gothic: Urus
Norse: Úr
Anglo-Saxon: Ur
Icelandic: Úr
Norwegian: Ur

Aurochs were a species of wild ox that lived in the European forests until they were hunted to extinction in the 1600's. This rune represents the cosmic seed, beginnings, and origins. It is masculine in nature and gives strength, endurance and athleticism. It is a rune of courage and boldness, freedom, rebellion, and independence. Ur represents the horn or the erect phallus, resurrection, life after death, as well as coming, being and passing away.

Representing the transfer of energies, it is used for projecting or drawing in of energy. Repeated use of the rune will gradually increase the amounts of energy one can handle at any given time and helps in the growth of one's own reserves of power.

Stones associated with this rune are agate, epidote, fire agate, and diamond.

THURISAZ (Giants/Thorn)

Germanic: Thyth (Thurisaz)
Gothic: Thauris
Norse: Þurs
Anglo-Saxon: þorn
Icelandic: Þurs
Norwegian: Thurs

Thurisaz represents the Jotnar (giants) and is the rune of primal forces, destruction, conflict, and curses. Thurisaz also governs the making of tools, especially the tools of war. Use this rune to break down barriers, destroy, and transform. Chaos is the true nature of this rune, and a strong will and mind is needed to make proper use of it. This rune can be used in conjunction with other runes and spells for any number off manifestation purposes. The rune itself is constructed to visually represent a thorn, a phallic symbol, as this rune represents masculine energies and can be used in virility or impotence rituals. This rune is highly effective when used with a bloodstone and used in conjunction with hematite can be very effective in deflecting curses.

Stones associated with this rune are bloodstone, hematite, cloudy quartz, agate, and malachite.

ANSUZ (Speech)

Germanic: Aza (Ansuz)
Gothic: Ansus
Norse: Óss, Áss
Anglo-Saxon: Aesc, (Os, Ac)
Icelandic: Óss, Áss

Ansuz is a rune that refers to speech and communication. The word 'Ansuz' is thought to mean 'mouth' which is meant to infer speech. The rune represents Odin, The All-Father, and is a rune of consciousness, mysticism, and mind. It opens channels of self-expression and overcomes obstacles of every kind. It can be used in initiating oneself with Odin and assists in enhancing one's psychic and magical abilities.

Ansuz also serves as a representation of breath, which can refer to the spirit. This rune is capable of evoking inspiration and is frequently used by artists and students of the occult. It has been found on many ancient artifacts, mainly staffs and rings which are presumed to have been imbued with the power of this rune.

This rune can have many practical implications such as rituals to be more confident and outspoken. Incorporate it in a ritual to help with any issues you might be having regarding speech, whether that be stage fright or anxiety around new people.

Stones associated with this rune are lapis lazuli, moldavite, opal, and kyanite.

RAIDHO (Riding)

Germanic: Reda (Raidho)
Gothic: Raida
Norse: Reið, Reiðr
Anglo-Saxon: Rad
Icelandic: Reið
Norwegian: Reid, Reidr

Raidho refers to travel, motion, and journeys. This rune is used to reveal the best way to proceed in a given situation and can illuminate the best path to take in our lives. In German 'Rad' means 'wheel', which is where this rune derives its name, and is also where the words 'road' and 'ride' come from. In addition, the Icelandic word for advice is 'Rada' and from these meanings we can surmise what this rune represents.

The construction of this rune is a combination of the Isa and an inverted Sowilo rune. The zig-zag shape represents a journey that changes directions, moving downward along the staff of the rune. Like Ansuz, Raidho is used to represent Odin, who was known as The Wanderer and The Rider. It is a rune of travel, journeys, and physical endurance, all of which Odin was known for. It has been used as a charm for travelers and as a guide for the dead in their journey to the afterlife. You can make your own charm to carry with you by etching, drawing, or painting this rune onto a piece of wood or stone. Raidho can also be included in any rituals pertaining to travel or change.

Stones associated with this rune are opal, quartz, Iolite (water sapphire), ametrine, dendritic agate and kyanite.

KENAZ (Torch)

Germanic: Chozma (Kenaz)
Gothic: Kaun
Norse: Kaun
Anglo-Saxon: Cen, Ken
Icelandic: Kaun
Norwegian: Kaun

The Kenaz rune represents our ability to harness the unseen forces of nature to illuminate our way, our ability to use the world around us to gain insight, wisdom, and security. While the Thurisaz rune represents tools, this rune represents what we're able to do with them. The torch that brightens the path before us and brings clarity to our past. This rune works great in conjunction with Ansuz when exploring ancestral connections and enlightenment. It is also the rune of feminine mysteries and knowledge and works wonderfully in any ritual involving feminine health and empowerment.

Stones associated with this rune are fire agate, fire opal, citrine, garnet, ruby sun stone and amber.

X

GEBO (Gift)

Germanic: Geuua (Gebo) Gothic Giba
Norse: Gipt, Giöf
Anglo-Saxon: Geofu (Gyfu)
Icelandic: Gjöf
Norwegian: Giof

Gebo is the rune of sacrifice and giving. A representation of something of personal value given freely, such as our blood when we choose to consecrate the runes in this way. This is a rune of initiation, where we make personal sacrifices to obtain knowledge, power, and wisdom such as when Odin hung from Yggdrasil for 9 days to attain knowledge.

Gebo can be utilized during any ceremony or ritual pertaining to harmony of a union, such as a contract or marriage. Gebo is also used in sex magic and as it is deeply tied to the exchange of energies between partners. Used with the Isa rune, the combination is powerful in binding enemies.

Stones associated with this rune are emerald and jade.

WUNJO (Joy)

Germanic: Uuinne (Wunjo)
Gothic: Winja
Norse: Vend
Anglo-Saxon: Wynn
Icelandic: Vin
Norwegian: Wynn

Wunjo is the rune of joy, used to bind us with those we care for and for strengthening those bonds. It is a rune of harmony, friendship, community, and family. Wunjo has the ability to banish the hurdles that foment alienation and prevent us from bonding. Use Wunjo as a ward to prevent the sorrows that would keep you from achieving your maximum level of consciousness. Community is the embodiment of this rune and all the things that make up that community: love, trust, health, and divine will.

Wunjo is commonly known as a rune of perfection and correct wishing. We can utilize the power of Wunjo to marry our dreams to our actions to achieve our maximum potential.

Stones associated with this rune are topaz and clear quartz.

HAGALAZ (Hail)

Germanic: Haal (Hagalaz) Gothic Hagl
Norse: Hagall
Anglo-Saxon: Hægl
Icelandic: Hagall
Norwegian: Hagall, Hagl

This rune represents hailstones and involuntary sacrifice with no reward. It is a rune of suffering and injustice. A rune of destruction, disaster and catastrophe. This rune is often used in black magic, sending destruction in the form of whatever runes and intentions are used with it, delivering violent loss and pain.

While this rune is typically used for harmful reasons, it can also be used to gain understanding of what we cannot control. It symbolizes fate and can be used to gain insight into our divine nature and the will of the gods. Use this rune in conjunction with other relevant runes to discover what fate has in store for you or others in trying times. For example, you can gain insight on the outcome of family ordeals by pairing this rune with Wunjo. In addition, you can attempt to alter fate by pairing this rune with Nauthiz and communing with the Norns who have power over the fates of humanity.

Stones associated with this rune are ruby, aquamarine, onyx and cassiterite.

NAUTHIZ (Necessity)

Germanic name: Noicz (Nauthiz)
Norse name: Nauð, Nauðr
Anglo-Saxon name: Nied (Nyd)
Icelandic name: Nauð
Norwegian name: Naudr, Naud

Nauthiz is the rune of endurance, will, and the mental strength needed to last. It represents the dark night of the soul and is connected to the Hagl rune. Nauthiz can be utilized to realize what we need in spite of what we desire. It has the ability to empower us with the wisdom to see what must be done in otherwise difficult situations.

When used in white magic, this rune gives defiance and the strength to carry on when all hope seems lost. It is a rune of survival and fearlessness in the face of death. When directed at another, this rune can give the spiritual strength to carry on and endure in the face of disaster.

Stones associated with this rune are obsidian, apatite, carnelian and azurite.

ISA (Ice)

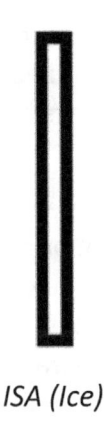

Germanic: Icz (Isa)
Gothic Eis
Norse: Íss
Anglo-Saxon: Is
Icelandic: Íss
Norwegian: Is

Isa is a rune of binding. It represents stealth and is used in operations where one wishes to proceed undetected by spiritual or physical entities.

In nature, ice creeps up on the land, quietly freezing and immobilizing everything in its path while the unaware fall victim to it. Isa the rune of binding and preventing action through hidden means. It can halt a plan and prevent something from developing. It is used to conceal and can render the victim unaware of impending personal disaster to the extent that any actions attempted will be too late in coming. It is also used in preventing any action from a known hostile party. Isa freezes action and is the rune of cold, barren stillness, and death. Isa is the polar opposite of Fehu, as Fehu is a rune of movement and Isa is a rune of binding.

This rune is helpful in meditation as it acts to still the mind and help concentration, bringing calmness and guidance. Isa works to calm hysteria, hyperactivity, and restlessness. Often used in protective spells to bind an aggressor, it also helps focus the will of the operator. Used with other runes, it acts to bind and shield the energies to keep them from interacting with each other.

Stones associated with this rune are malachite, obsidian, smoky quartz, and diamond.

JERA (Year)

Germanic name: Gaar (Jera)
Gothic: Jer
Norse: Ár
Anglo-Saxon: Ger (Jara)
Icelandic: Ár
Norwegian: Jara, Ar

Jera is a rune of cycles and is symbolic of the harvest where the efforts of planting and working in the fields are rewarded with crops. Ar represents the cycles of change, including life cycles, lunar cycles, and the seasons. Jera is in contrast to Isa where everything stops. It signifies the return of the Sun and brings action. Jera symbolizes a vortex of cycling energy: the eight-fold wheel of life, the point inside of the circle, which is the glyph for the Sun, meaning regeneration. Jera can bring a reversal of personal fortunes. Like the tarot card, the Wheel of Fortune, Jera can reverse circumstances, so misfortune is replaced with luck and visa-versa.

Jera is the rune of patience and awareness, moving in harmony with natural cycles. It is excellent for working with nature and is a rune of fruitfulness. Ingwaz is the seed planted, Berkano is the earth that receives it and Jera is the growth and the harvest. It is a rune of long-term planning and persistence that helps ensure the success of plans.

Stones associated with this rune are moss agate, lepidolite, and moonstone.

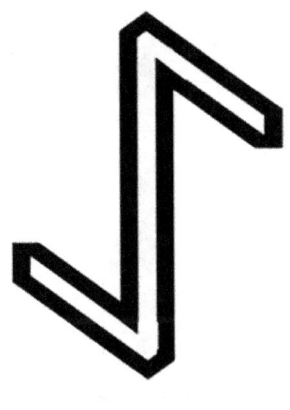

EIHWAZ (Yew Tree)

Germanic name: Ezck (Eihwaz)
Gothic: Eihwas
Norse: Elhaz
Anglo-Saxon: Yr (Ēoh)
Norwegian: Eo

The Eihwaz rune represents the yew: the tree of life and death. This rune is frequently compared to the death tarot and holds many of the same meanings. Eihwaz is a rune of transformation, death and the beginning of something new. Eihwaz can represent the reversal of a current situation, or the beginning of something new coming from the ashes of old habits or attachments. Eihwaz is designed to show the duality that is life and death and their inseparable connection. Eihwaz reminds us to not fear death. It is merely a part of the cycle of life and rebirth and should be welcomed as it heralds change and new beginnings.

Stones associated with this rune are aquamarine, gold stones, and chrysocolla.

PERTHRO (Unknown)

Germanic name: Pertra (Perthro)
Gothic: Pairthra
Norse: Perð
Anglo-Saxon: Peordh (Pertra)
Icelandic: Perð, (Plástur)
Norwegian: (Pertra)

Perthro is a rune of divination. The unknown represents our fate and the control one has over their life. Our fates are tied to our actions and luck, and with divination we can ask The Norns to give us a glimpse into what may be if we remain on our current course.

Perthro is the most mysterious of runes as it deals with the mysteries of the other runes, life itself and our relationship with them. Fate, chance, and action are undeniably linked, creating a web between ourselves, the gods, and the universe. This rune ultimately represents these links and can be used for divination purposes in conjunction with other runes or by itself to ask favor and insight from the Spinners of Fate.

Stones associated with this rune are onyx, amethyst, labradorite, and sapphire.

ALGIZ (Life)

Germanic name: Algis, Algiz or Elhaz
Gothic: Algs
Anglo-Saxon name: Eolh
Norwegian name: Elgr

Algiz is the rune of life. It is constructed in a way as to represent three branches atop the World Pillar, symbolic of a tree reaching up towards the heavens. It is a powerful rune of protection and represents the greatest defense that exists in the futhark runes, the branches represent the horns of an elk which are able to attack as well as defend.

Algiz can be used as a shield against spiritual and physical attacks. It represents the power of man and their divine fate to uphold the order created by the gods in defense of Asgard and Midgard. It is also used in consecration and the banishing of negative energies. It is excellent for witches to wear when performing dangerous rituals as it protects against wayward disruptive energy. It can also be carved into an object and placed upon an altar or spell-space.

Stones related to this rune are amethyst, emerald, fire agate, yellow jasper, smoky quartz, kunzite, labradorite and obsidian.

SOWILO (Sun)

Germanic: Sugil (Sowilo)
Gothic: Sauil
Norse: Sól
Anglo-Saxon: Sigel
Icelandic: Sól
Norwegian: Sol Old
Danish: Sulu
Old German: Sil, Sigo, Sulhil

The rune of the Sun and the counterforce to Isa, the rune of Ice. Sowilo is a rune of action, honor, invincibility, and final triumph. It is the rune of movement that bestows the will to act. It symbolizes the chakras and the lightning bolt, the spark of life. It has both shielding and combative properties. It is used for understanding the energy forces in the world and on the astral plane. When used with other runes, it activates and empowers them. It can be used in meditation and to empower your own stores of energy. Sowilo brings out one's leadership abilities and enhances one's strength of spirit.

Stones associated with this gem are ruby, red spinel, red garnet, rubellite, and diamond.

TIWAZ (Tyr)

Germanic: Tys (Tiwaz)
Gothic: Teiws
Norse: Týr
Anglo-Saxon: Tir, Tiw
Icelandic: Týr
Norwegian: Ty

The Tiwaz rune is associated with Tyr, the sky god of justice. The rune is constructed in a way to represent a balanced spear-point which indicates movement in a single or upward direction. This rune also represents sacrifice as Tyr sacrificed his hand to bind the wolf of chaos, Fenrir.

Tiwaz is the rune of harmony, justice and the warrior. It represents honor, which is representative of the sacrifice Tyr made to uphold the cosmic order. It is used for stability and the binding of chaotic energies. It is good for defense and revenge workings as it represents justice.

Stones associated with this rune are hematite, sunstone, bloodstone, tiger eye, and heliotrope.

BERKANO (Birch Goddess)

Germanic: Bercna (Berkano)
Gothic: Bairkan
Norse: Bjarkan
Anglo-Saxon: Beroc
Icelandic: Bjarkan
Norwegian: Bjarkan

Berkano gets its name from the birch tree which represents regeneration and youth. The rune alludes to the female form and is constructed to represent the breasts and belly of a pregnant woman. Berkano represents birth and rebirth after destruction. It is commonly associated with Ostara, goddess of spring and rebirth.

This rune can be used in workings for female fertility, feminine magic, and nurturing. It is also used in concealment and protection. This rune symbolizes feminine energies and it is an old pagan custom to enclose a child at birth with the protective energies of Berkano, which remain with them throughout their lives. Berkano is also an excellent rune to utilize when farming and gardening, for example you could paint the Berkano rune on a large rock and place it in the center of your garden while asking the goddess to watch over your crop.

Stones associated with this rune are rose quartz, garnet, agate, and clear quartz.

EHWAZ (Horse)

Germanic: Eys (Ehwaz)
Gothic: Aihwa
Norse: Ehol, Ior
Anglo-Saxon: Eoh
Icelandic: Eykur
Norwegian: Eh, Eol

This rune represents the horse and is constructed in a way to appear as two horses facing one another, an allusion to the horses Árvakr and Alsviðr pulling the chariot of the Sun. It is also closely identified with Castor and Pollux, the Gemini twins. Ehwaz represents the duality of the masculine and feminine and mankind's ability to work together to achieve a common goal.

Ehwaz can be used to bless new partnerships and coalitions, whether that be marriage, friendships, group projects or the creation of alliances. When used with other runes Eihwaz unites the energies harmoniously.

Stones that are associated with this rune are agate, chrysoprase, citrine, moonstone, pear, and white sapphire.

MANNAZ (Mankind)

Germanic: Manna (Mannaz)
Gothic: Manna
Norse: Maðr
Anglo-Saxon: Mann
Icelandic: Maður
Norwegian: Madr

Mannaz represents the link between mankind and the gods, our shared ability of mind and memory that lead us to great things. Mannaz has a type of twisting in its structure, representing how the fates of mankind and the gods are intertwined and cannot be undone. The shape of the rune is two Wunjo runes facing one another, one representing man and the other the gods.

The Mannaz rune is often used in prophetic magic and can be utilized to commune with and honor the gods. It is a rune of destiny, fate, and potential and can be used attain wisdom and better understand out place in the universe amongst the grand order of things.

Stones that are associated with this rune are sapphire, celestite, agate, moonstone, and tiger's eye.

Laguz (Water)

Germanic: Laaz (Laguz)
Gothic: Lagus
Norse: Lögr
Anglo-Saxon: Lagu
Icelandic: Lögur
Norwegian: Laukr

Laguz is a rune that is meant to symbolize downward flowing water that is full of energy. It also represents the concept of quantity as opposed to quality. The downward slope in the rune represents water flowing downhill. Laguz also represents unbridled chaotic energy and the erosive forces of nature. It is a rune of becoming, a rune of progress and collective forces.

Laguz is a great rune to incorporate into any ritual that grants endurance and willpower, especially rituals that help with setting and achieving goals.

Stones associated with this rune are lapis lazuli, azurite, amethyst, aquamarine and sapphire.

INGWAZ (Seed)

Norse: Ing, Ingvarr
Gothic: Iggws
Germanic: Enguz (Ingwaz)
Anglo-Saxon: Ing
Icelandic: Ing
Norwegian: Ing

Ingwaz is the rune of isolation, used for preparing a space for new growth to begin. It is the rune of gestation and internal growth. It represents the ancient image of God, Ing, and is the rune of male fertility. Creative action, stored energy, and power from meditation are all good examples of Ing, it is a rune of action and everything needed to perform that action. The idea of sacrifice is a core component of Ingwaz: for something new to come about there must be something that is let go - an internal or external change must occur, this might manifest in the form of time lost as you learn a new skill or study for an exam or it might mean in order for you to grow you have to separate yourself from a person or group of people.

One of the main reasons a spell or ritual might fail is the failure of the practitioner to make the necessary sacrifices to achieve their goals and Ingwaz can help us understand what they might be. Use this rune as part of a pre-casting meditation ritual to better understand what is needed from you for your manifestation to be successful. Another great way to utilize this rune is for the purposes of separating your mind from distraction to focus on the task at hand.

Stones associated with this rune are zircon, peridot, prehnite, and tanzanite.

DAGAZ (Dawn)

Germanic: Daaz (Dagaz)
Gothic: Dags
Norse: Dagr
Anglo-Saxon: Daeg
Icelandic: Dagur
Norwegian: Dagr

The counterpart to the Jera rune, Dagaz represents the daily cycle in the same way that Jera represents the yearly cycle. Both are runes of change. Dagaz is the rune of spiritual awakening and is a symbol of light. The construction of the rune is that of an infinity symbol or an overturned hourglass, representing timelessness and limitless potential.

This rune is used to attain inspiration and enlightenment. Meditate with this rune to discover the answers to problems or blocks you've been facing. As its name entails, Dagaz can shine light on an otherwise ambiguous situation and can be useful in any ritual involving answers and understanding.

Stones associated with this rune are lapis lazuli, moonstone, sunstone, ruby, and jade.

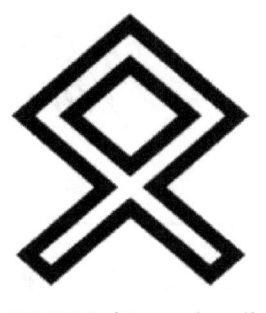

OTHALA (Homeland)

Germanic: Utal (Othala)
Gothic: Othal
Norse: Oðal
Anglo-Saxon: Otael (Ethel)
Icelandic: Óðal
Norwegian: Ödal

Othala governs any matter dealing with ancestry, inheritance, family and estate. Similar to Fehu, it is a rune of wealth and property but where Fehu represents the beginnings of wealth and its transformation over time, Othala represents immovable wealth that has been generated by your ancestral line to be passed down to newer generations.

Othala can be used to celebrate the lives of our ancestors, praise their accomplishments and bless the legacies they left behind to help us carry on their names.

Stones associated with this rune are citron, green jade, tigers eye, rose quartz

Notes

In Closing

I hope you enjoyed my *Book of Shadows*! The world of magic is vast and there is a seemingly limitless wealth of information on countless topics so let this book be a steppingstone on your own spiritual path. If you enjoyed this book check out my beginner witchcraft book *The Craft,* it's full of information regarding the history and current practices of modern witchcraft.

If you have a moment, please leave a review for the book on Amazon! I self-publish all my books and it really helps as I don't have a publisher advertising my content. Thank you for reading my book and blessed be!

Merry met!
And merry part!
-Brittany Nightshade

Disclaimer: Always take safety precautions when doing any ritual. Be careful if using stoves or any heat sources and always make sure to have proper ventilation. This information is educational and religious, it is not to be taken as professional medical advice, always consult with a medical professional first and foremost. Use this book at your own peril: I'm not responsible for any unintended consequences. Never ingest anything unless you're completely sure it's safe and you aren't allergic. Always be wary of the potential risk of forcing your will onto others, as there can be unintended consequences. Do not commit any crimes, such as trespassing, when conducting your rituals: I don't have a spell to get you out of jail!

Much love,
Brittany

If you've enjoyed the book, please consider giving me a review on Amazon and following me on Instagram and Facebook:

facebook.com/xobrittanynightshade
@Nightshade_Apothecary